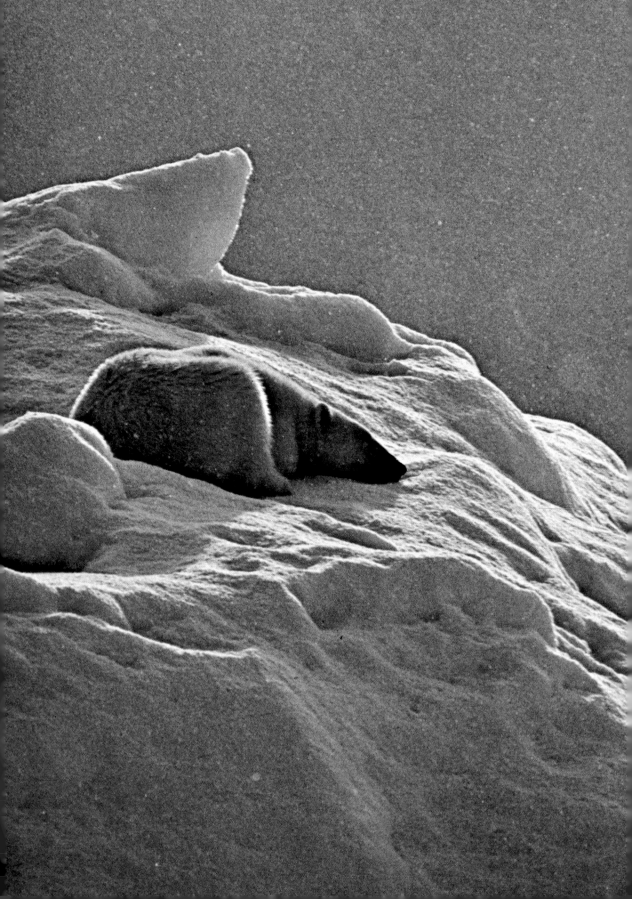

G. Carleton Ray and M. G. McCormick-Ray

A Chanticleer Press Edition

WILDLIFE OF THE POLAR REGIONS

HARRY N. ABRAMS, INC., PUBLISHERS, NEW YORK

First frontispiece. *An ermine, or short-tailed weasel* (Mustela erminea), *is camouflaged in snow. Ermines range from the northern tier of the North Temperate Zone to the high Arctic.*

Second frontispiece. *In the dim glow of sunset, a snowy owl* (Nyctea scandiaca) *surveys the wintry tundra of Canada's Northwest Territories.*

Third frontispiece. *A polar bear* (Ursus maritimus) *rests on the island of Spitzbergen. These bears spend most of their lives roaming the ice pack.*

Overleaf. *Adélie penguins* (Pygoscelis adeliae) *gather on the ice of the Antarctic shore.*

Library of Congress Cataloging in Publication Data

Ray, G. Carleton.
Wildlife of the polar regions.
(Wildlife habitat series)
"A Chanticleer Press edition."
Includes index.
1. Zoology—Polar regions. 2. Botany—Polar regions. I. McCormick-Ray, M. G., joint author. II. Title.
QL84.75.R39   574.998   81-5069
ISBN 0-8109-1768-8   AACR2

Color reproductions by Fontana & Bonomi, Milan, Italy
Composition by Dix Typesetting Co. Inc., Syracuse, N.Y.
Printed and bound by Kingsport Press, Kingsport, Tennessee

Prepared and produced by Chanticleer Press, Inc., New York:
Publisher: Paul Steiner
Editor-in-Chief: Milton Rugoff
Managing Editor: Gudrun Buettner
Series Editor: Mary Suffudy
Natural Science Editor: John Farrand, Jr.
Assistant Editor: Nancy Hornick
Marketing: Carol Robertson
Production: Helga Lose, Dean Gibson
Art Associates: Carol Nehring, Art Bonanno
Picture Librarians: Joan Lynch, Edward Douglas
Drawings: Dolores R. Santoliquido
Series Design: Massimo Vignelli

Editorial Consultant: Edward R. Ricciuti
Scientific Consultant: Francis S. L. Williamson, Chief Scientist, Office of Polar Programs, Smithsonian Institution

Appendix text: pp. 194–197, 202–217 by Joseph R. Jehl, Jr., Hubbs Sea World Research Institute; pp. 218–221 by Guido Dingerkus, Department of Ichthyology, American Museum of Natural History; pp. 198–199, 222-225 by Michael Neushul, Professor of Marine Botany, University of California, Santa Barbara; pp. 200–201 by David L. Pawson, Department of Invertebrate Zoology, National Museum of Natural History, Smithsonian Institution.

Note: Illustrations are numbered according to the pages on which they appear.

Contents

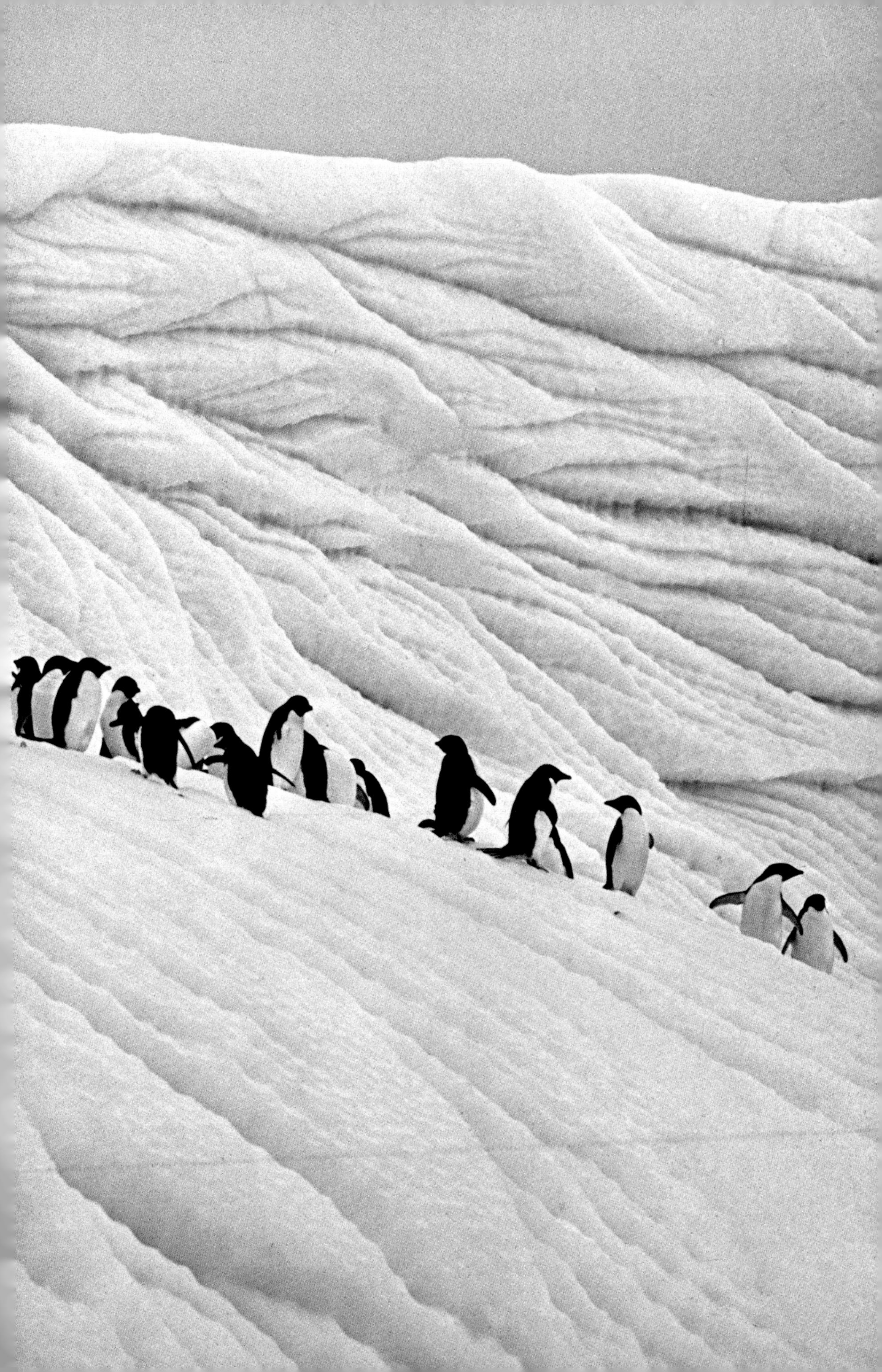

Preface

The age of exploration and discovery still goes on at the top and bottom of the world—those ice-dominated places which we call the polar regions. There, more than anywhere else on Earth, we have a sense of newness, of a freedom from pollution and the tragic pressure of overpopulation, and of a chance for civilization to husband its resources wisely.

Man has never inhabited the south polar region called the Antarctic and, though native peoples have lived in the Arctic for a long time, only recently has modern technology allowed man to penetrate to both poles and into—and beneath—ice-covered polar seas. Now we can only hope that our mistakes in exploiting other regions of the Earth will not be repeated there.

It surprises most people to learn that the polar regions contain the largest remaining pools of resources—both living and non-living—that have not been intensively exploited. Both polar regions have already suffered abuse, most notably in the depletion of seals, whales, and sea otters, but none of these has become extinct. There is much left and the ecosystems are still largely intact. We may still save them.

We are fortunately abandoning the old view of the polar regions as the vast "wastes" that journalistic clichés sometimes paint them. These "wastes," we now know, contain the largest flocks of birds, the largest aggregations of mammals, and the largest plankton swarms known. True, there is not as great a total diversity of life as in warmer places, but many species live nowhere else, being exquisitely adapted to the ice age climate in which we still live. No regions have such wide seasonal fluctuations or such long nights in winter, but the summer flowers on the tundra are charming, and the night skies are mostly clear and brilliantly lit by stars and sometimes by spectacular auroras.

We who have had special opportunities to experience the polar regions first hand have other pleasant memories: the thrill of discovering the Alaskan snow flea while living on a snow field, of diving with Antarctic Weddell seals, of training—or being trained by—those greatest of polar predators, killer whales, of going out in skin boats with Eskimos as they hunted walruses, seals, and bowhead whales among the ice of the Bering Sea. Those experiences are woven into the fabric of this book.

Of course, no one could possibly cover more than a part of what we may call the "polar experience." We are confined, too, by the limits of existing knowledge. Thus we have not said more of those fascinating Antarctic fishes, the notothenioids—for which there is not yet even a vernacular name—largely because most of their behavior and ecology remain to be discovered. Even well-known animals and phenomena require further research. For example, the explanation of the lemming's population fluctuations are still only hypothetical. And how the common Alaska blackfish can withstand freezing cold is but partly known. What we still experience in the polar regions is a sense of newness, a sense of wonder at how little we know. The questions excite us more than the answers.

The large, warm-blooded vertebrates—birds and mammals—the best known and most photographed of polar wildlife, are understandably featured in this book.

This emphasis is not meant to suggest that the diatoms, plankton, fish, soil microbes, benthic fauna, and so forth, are less important. In terms of the functioning of polar ecosystems they may be more so, indeed, in terms of their life histories, these lesser beasts and plants are even more astonishing. Among the better-known species, we have chosen to speak mostly of animals that are primarily or uniquely polar as compared with immigrants: the polar regions contain many "invaders" from temperate climes, particularly in summer. We have also chosen to discuss emergent knowledge and more or less newly discovered patterns such as food webs and resource partitioning. Why is it important that we know about—and care for— the polar regions? Simply because the conflicts between the use of resources there may soon become intense. Can we afford to fish for krill and at the same time hope that krill-eating whales will return to their former abundance? Can we drill for oil in the seas of these regions without grave consequences for the stability of the sea ice cover which exerts a major influence on the Earth's climate? We must, in other words, consider the consequences of our actions. Human civilization depends as much on nature's ecosystems as does any animal or plant. Knowledge, as well as sympathy, is required for the care we now must increasingly show for nature.

This book is the work of many caring hands and minds. To Milton Rugoff, Gudrun Buettner, Mary Suffudy, Nancy Hornick, and the entire staff of Chanticleer Press who worked with us we extend special thanks. We also thank Dr. Francis S. L. Williamson who reviewed and made valuable comments on the manuscript, and those several contributors who wrote captions and appendixes, as credited on the copyright page. Without all of these people, this book could not have been written.

G. Carleton Ray and M. G. McCormick-Ray

Shimmering and dancing in the northern sky, polar auroras appear as draperies, bands, and other designs of light. These northern lights (or aurora borealis) and southern lights (or aurora australis) occur during all seasons, but, like stars, are visible only when skies are dark. The auroras are produced when streams of electrons and protons from space travel along the Earth's magnetic lines and concentrate in belts surrounding the magnetic poles. These electrons and protons excite atmospheric gases, producing the magnificent displays.

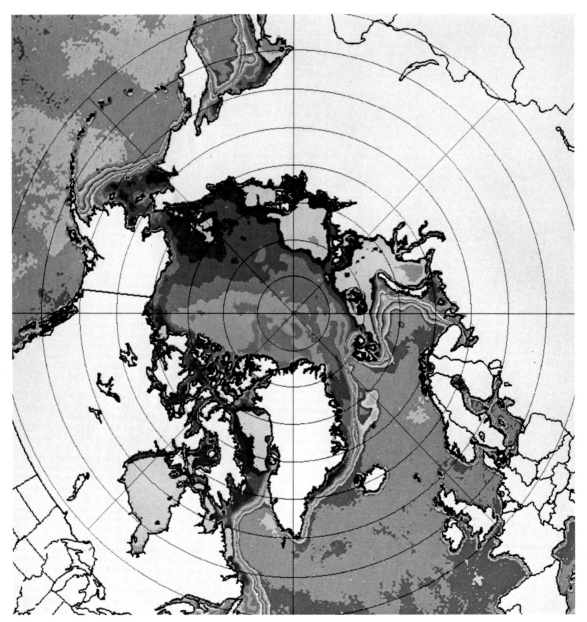

280K	205K
275K	200K
270K	195K
265K	190K
260K	185K
255K	180K
250K	175K
245K	170K
240K	165K
235K	160K
230K	155K
225K	150K
220K	145K
215K	140K
210K	135K

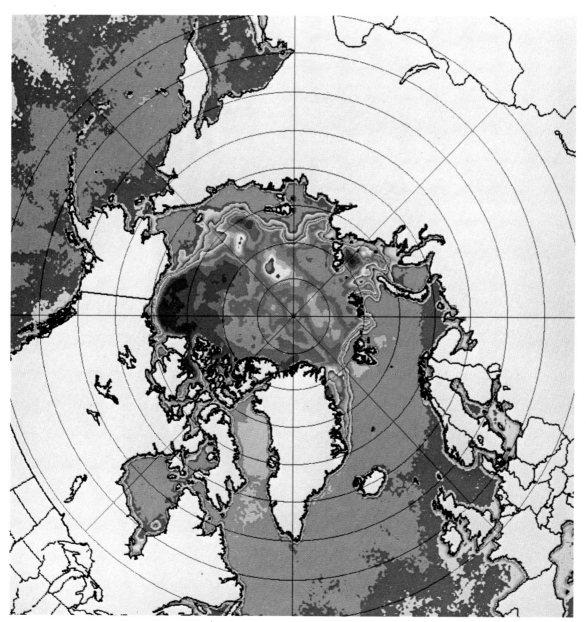

This computer simulation of microwave radiation measured by the Nimbus 5 satellite shows the differences in the extent of Arctic sea ice cover in winter (14) and summer (above). Land, sea ice, and the ocean all emit microwave radiation, but to differing degrees. Land has the highest emission, ice somewhat less, and the ocean least, because the surface of the ocean reflects the microwaves back into the water. The emissions are measured in terms of brightness temperature. The color corresponding to 150° Kelvin represents ice that is just forming, constituting 15 percent ice cover. At 235° Kelvin, the ice cover is 100 percent. Note that the greatest contrast in color is at the ice edge, where the sea ice meets open water.

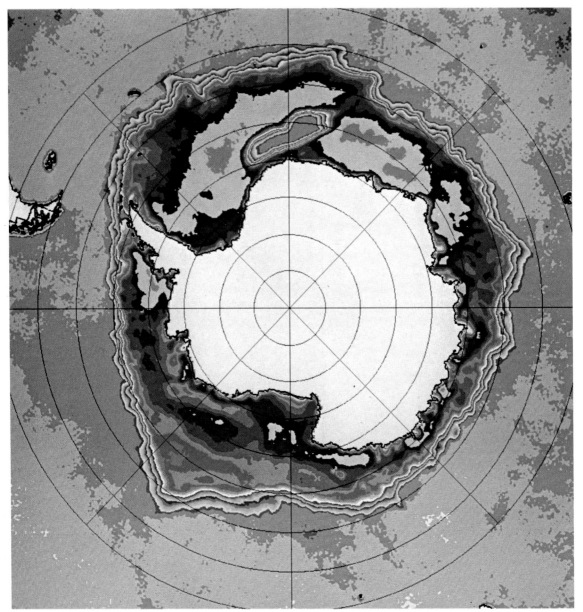

280K	205K
275K	200K
270K	195K
265K	190K
260K	185K
255K	180K
250K	175K
245K	170K
240K	165K
235K	160K
230K	155K
225K	150K
220K	145K
215K	140K
210K	135K

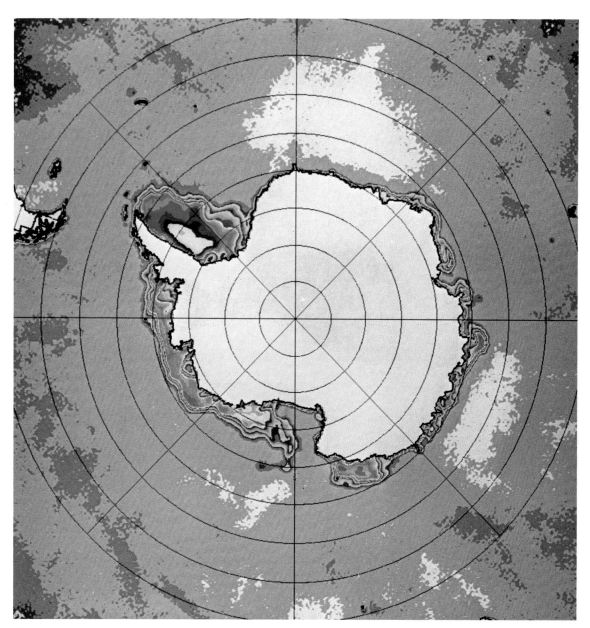

Computer simulations of
microwave radiation show the
seasonal differences in the extent
of sea ice surrounding the
Antarctic mainland, depicted in
white. In the photograph taken
during the austral winter (16),
one sees large areas of ice that are
almost or fully formed,
corresponding to temperatures
around 235° Kelvin. Ice
completely surrounds the
continent. There is little ice of
this type in the summer photo
(above). The ice represented by
light blue forms far from the
mainland in winter, but fringes
the continent in summer. The
seasonal change is dramatic in
the Antarctic, where ice expands
into the surrounding oceans; in
the Arctic ice is relatively
confined by landmasses that
surround the Arctic Ocean.

An Age of Ice

"Polar wastes"—how often we encounter this misleading cliché and how easily we accept its dismal implications. The term "polar regions" brings to mind images of a vast frozen ground, of icebergs, glaciers, and freezing seas. It suggests food paucity, cold, discomfort, scarce wildlife, and few human settlements. But the true nature of polar regions is very different from this.

In fact, it is precisely because of the dominance of ice and snow in these regions that they are so important to man. The polar regions are a vital component in the mechanisms that control the climatic conditions to which life on Earth has become adjusted. Beyond that, the largest unexploited living resources left on Earth are found in the rich polar seas. We may also be challenged by such intriguing questions as how life has evolved and maintained itself there. For, though the polar regions may not be so diverse in species of many groups as are other regions, we may well ask: How have organisms adapted to them and how can such relatively simple ecosystems be so productive?

Only recently has man learned that the polar regions contain productive ecosystems. The history of polar exploration is relatively brief. Man has occupied the Arctic region for several millennia, but the first man ever to spend a season on continental Antarctica did so only at the turn of this century. And detailed scientific research did not begin until the establishment of permanent polar and subpolar research stations after World War II. We now know that while the physical nature of the polar regions sets stringent demands for life and produces a deceptively simple ecological setting, these regions support enormous swarms of plankton (floating plant and animal organisms), the largest populations of seabirds in the world, whales, walruses, seals, polar bears, and great herds of caribou—obviously not a "wasteland" at all!

On the other hand, whole groups of animals and plants have not yet adapted to polar conditions. No amphibian (frog, toad, or salamander) or reptile (snake, lizard, or turtle) inhabits the treeless polar regions. No truly terrestrial vertebrates and no ferns, gymnosperms, or freshwater fishes are found on continental Antarctica. In fact, only about 4 percent of the Antarctic land mass supports life, and this life is largely composed of a few microbes, protozoans, rotifers, spiders and their relatives, insects, mosses, fungi, algae, and lichens. In the Arctic as well, terrestrial life forms are relatively few, though vastly richer than on Antarctica in terms of both numbers of species and biomass (weight of living matter per unit of living area). For example, only two dozen or so of about 3,200 mammal species in the world inhabit the area north of the treeline—the northern limit of tree growth—in North America. By contrast, there are two to three times that number in several midwestern states of temperate North America, and six times that number in some small tropical Central American countries. The low polar diversity of some groups of plant and animal life, some scientists believe, is related to the youth, geologically speaking, of polar ecosystems.

But one should not think of polar regions only in terms of harsh conditions and paucity of species. The spring season, however brief, brings vitality and abundance just as elsewhere on Earth, but much more suddenly. Arctic

oceanic waters over continental shelves bloom with plankton that form a rich bouillabaisse of life that may go unnoticed by the untrained eye, but not by fish, birds, seals, and whales. Spring in the Arctic brings overflowing rivers and opens up an abundance of freshwater lakes. The warming sun brings about changes that awaken dormant organisms and the lengthening days to the south prompt migrants, such as waterfowl, to return to their summer homes to rear young. As summer progresses, insects and flowers emerge, including those notorious bloodsuckers, the tiny "no-see-em" flies, mosquitoes, and black flies—all a strain to man and wildlife.

There is an equally astonishing productivity in the waters of the Antarctic region. The great whales travel to this region to feed, and penguins and seals find a rich source of food there. The Antarctic region's Southern Ocean may cover only about 5 percent of the Earth's ocean surface, but it can average four times the productivity of other oceans. According to one estimate, the Southern Ocean produces 20 percent of all oceanic living material annually. No wonder the world is looking at a little crustacean called krill (*Euphausia superba*), which this ocean so abundantly produces, as a source of food and fertilizer.

What Are the Polar Regions?
Before we describe the extent of these regions we must define some terms. The poles are not regions but only points through which the Earth's axis runs. The Arctic region and the Antarctic region, on the other hand, are the two climatically defined areas surrounding the North Pole and the South Pole. Antarctica refers to the continent at the center of the Antarctic region; it is surrounded by the Southern Ocean. The Arctic region is the opposite of the Antarctic region. At its center is the Arctic Ocean, and it is surrounded by the great land masses of Eurasia and North America.

The polar regions can be delineated by astronomical limits or by ecological conditions. The Arctic and Antarctic circles are determined by the astronomical positions of Earth and sun and by the tilt of the Earth on its axis. In the Northern Hemisphere on June 21, the sun is perpendicular to the surface of the Earth at the Tropic of Cancer, at 23° and 30 minutes north latitude, and its rays are tangential to the Antarctic Circle, at 66° and 33 minutes south latitude. Thus, for one whole day, all the area south of the Antarctic Circle receives no direct sunlight. From June 22 until December 21, as the Earth orbits the sun, the sun descends in northern skies. On September 21, the sun is perpendicular to the Equator; this is the fall equinox, a day when day and night lengths are exactly equal over the whole Earth—12 hours each—except at the poles where the sun rises and sets but once a year. Then, on December 21, the sun is farthest south, perpendicular to Earth at the Tropic of Capricorn, at 23° and 30 minutes south latitude; and its rays are tangential to the Earth at the Arctic Circle, at 66° and 33 minutes north latitude. Thus, for the 6 months of the sun's decline from northern skies, the loss of day length at the Arctic Circle has been almost eight minutes a day. Then from December 22 to June 21, the whole procedure is reversed.

Top. *A small group of Adélie penguins* (Pygoscelis adeliae) *rides on a chunk of Antarctic sea ice.*

Center. *The bearded seal* (Erignathus barbatus) *inhabits the pack ice of the Arctic. These animals shy away from shorefast ice, preferring loosely packed floes. There are perhaps 100,000 bearded seals in existence. Reaching a body length of more than 2½ meters, they are the largest hair seals of the Arctic.*

Bottom. *A lone Dominican gull* (Larus dominicanus) *perches on a small ice floe off Palmer Peninsula, Antarctica. Seabirds thrive in polar waters, because cold seas have an abundance of fish and invertebrates. Gulls do not dive, but seize their food near the surface.*

The sun travels north again, passing a spring equinox on March 21. It is important to keep in mind that 6-month days and nights—beginning and ending at the equinoxes—are features of the poles only and not of the entire polar regions, which extend well beyond those points. Their winter days may be short, but daylight is not totally absent. The summer days are gloriously long, and can be warm—even hot on the Arctic tundra because of these long periods of solar radiation.

In the winter, spectacular displays of red, yellow, and green light illuminate polar skies and can occasionally be seen in temperate regions—rarely in the tropics—as well. These are the northern lights, or aurora borealis, and the southern lights, or aurora australis. They, and bright moonlight, reflecting on snow, actually can make polar nights bright enough to read by. The auroras have been the source of legend. Northern Germanic tribes considered them to be the shields of the *Valkyrie* and medieval Europeans thought they warned of the plague. Some Eskimos thought they showed departed spirits kicking a walrus skull about. The Australian aborigines thought they told of a dance of the Gods and the Ceylonese regarded them as a message from Buddha. The auroras occur during all seasons, but like the stars, can only be seen when skies are dark. They are produced when streams of electrons and protons from space stream along the Earth's magnetic lines to concentrate in auroral belts surrounding the magnetic poles, there to excite atmospheric gasses which produce the auroral displays. Enormous amounts of energy are involved in these magnetic storms which are intensified during years of sunspots. No one yet knows if the auroras affect biological processes, but they are surely beautiful.

But polar life and ecological conditions do not follow strict astronomical delineations, except in a very general way. The environmental features that characterize the Antarctic and Arctic regions do not follow neat latitudinal lines. The approximately circular Southern Ocean, which surrounds Antarctica and also is continuous with the Atlantic, Pacific, and Indian oceans at their southern extremities, is defined by a temperature and salinity change that separates the cold Antarctic surface waters sharply from more northerly waters. Cold, northward-flowing surface waters of the Southern Ocean meet warmer, southward-flowing surface waters at the Antarctic convergence between 50° to 60° south latitude. This convergence is a barrier that confines the distributions of many species to produce the unique community structure of the Southern Ocean. Of course, many larger animals such as the great whales do cross this barrier easily.

Some scientists would greatly increase the size of the Southern Ocean by noting the existence of another temperature and salinity change at about 40° south latitude. This is the subtropical convergence. Whereas all surface waters south of the Antarctic convergence have temperatures from about −2° to +2° C, there is an abrupt temperature rise at the Antarctic convergence to approximately 6° C, and a gradual increase to 10° C at the subtropical convergence. To include all waters south of the subtropical convergence—the northernmost extent of

Overleaf. *During the summer, vast amounts of fresh water from rivers and melting snow and ice flow into the ocean from the adjacent continent. Consequently, Arctic seas are covered with a layer of relatively dilute saline water.*

drifting Antarctic icebergs—would increase the size of the Southern Ocean to 75 million square kilometers or 22 percent of all oceans, six times Antarctica itself, and three times the size of the Arctic region. Still, even this immense area holds but 10 percent of the world ocean's heat, which is important for the heat balance of the Earth. We shall define the Antarctic region as encompassing the seas south of the Antarctic convergence, including some distinctive oceanic, subantarctic islands, though such a precise definition is not agreed upon by all ecologists and oceanographers.

Defining the extent of the Arctic region is even more complex. Both land and sea areas are included, and different definitions must be used for each. First, it has been a matter of convenience to consider 10° C during the warmest month as the upper mean temperature limit for many forms of polar life.

Therefore, the 10° isotherm—a line which includes all areas of a mean monthly temperature of 10° or less during the warmest month—should define the Arctic region. Such a line wavers about 70° north latitude from Norway through Siberia and from Alaska through westernmost Canada. But for both oceanographic and geographic reasons, the line dips to 50° north latitude to include the Bering Sea and most of northern Canada and Greenland. The matter is still more complicated by the fact that treeless tundra and the frozen ground called permafrost must be included. This extends the Arctic region to include more southerly areas of western Alaska, northern Canada, and Siberia. At best, however, this is but a rough approximation, in contrast to the more precise and convenient Antarctic convergence, for which there is no northern counterpart.

Altitudinal variations make the picture even more complex. For example, polar equivalents exist on mountains, even at the Equator. Climbing a mountain is analogous to going poleward. The reason is that for every 1,000-meter gain in altitude, temperature drops about 3°. This is like traveling about 540 kilometers poleward. Put another way, a 3,000-meter mountain top in the Rockies or Alps is climatically much like the Arctic. This is why some of the species found on Arctic tundra, that were formerly more widespread, continue to exist in the Alps, the Rockies, and elsewhere.

Thus, as we have defined it, the Antarctic region is larger and rounder than the irregularly shaped Arctic region. Also, because the Antarctic region is composed of a continent surrounded by water and the Arctic is a sea surrounded by continents, the distributions and communities of wildlife are quite different in the two polar regions. The North Pole lies near the center of a great ocean basin, thinly covered with ice at sea level, and the South Pole is located on a land mass, thickly covered with glacial ice, 2,912 meters high, and dry. The Arctic Ocean is more or less cut off from other ocean waters whereas the Southern Ocean unites the three other great oceans— Atlantic, Pacific, and Indian. The Arctic is surrounded by the continents of Eurasia and North America, whereas Antarctica is separated from all other land masses by a cold and often violent sea. The Arctic has a great many rivers, a fact with profound consequences for life and the mechanisms of productivity, while the Antarctic is nearly

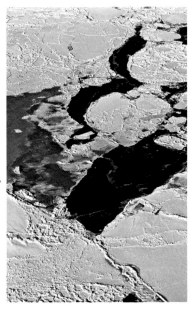

devoid of them. The continental shelves of the Arctic are the world's widest, but those of Antarctica are relatively narrow and the deepest on Earth, their edges reaching depths of 1,000 meters.

In spite of all these differences, there are great similarities between the two regions and remarkable parallelisms and convergences in the evolution of life on these ends of the planet Earth. Both regions are harshly cold in winter, and both contain vast deserts, burdened by ice and pierced by mountain peaks called *nunataks*. But both also bear witness to great productivity during brief summers, and they experience great fluctuations between seasons, the variations in temperature and light being the greatest on Earth.

Historical Perspective

The polar regions have not always been as we know them today. Over the Earth's 4-billion-year history, great changes have occurred in the present locations and distributions of land masses, in the positions of the magnetic and axial poles, in the presence and extent of ice cover, and in the evolution and distribution of life. Furthermore, the Earth's present climate, which truly represents an "ice age," has not been the normal situation for our planet. Periods of such massive glaciation as now exists—even more massive 20,000 years ago—have probably occurred only four times on Earth: in the Precambrian, about 600 million years ago; in the late Ordovician, about 450 million years ago; in the late Carboniferous to early Permian, about 300 to 250 million years ago; and in the late Cenozoic, from about 4 million years ago (in the Arctic) and 40 million years ago (in the Antarctic) to the present. Those glaciations have had profound effects on sea level, climate, and life, but they may have been present during less than 20 percent of the last half billion years. So, we now live in a rather special time, and, if the 50-million-year Permian glaciation is an example, we may have just begun our present Ice Age.

The Earth's seven continents originated from one supercontinent called Pangaea, but the position of the poles relative to this great land mass was not always constant. For example, from the Devonian to the Carboniferous period, the center of Pangaea was almost surely not polar, as concluded by scientists on the basis of studies of both geology and the Earth's magnetism. Recent studies of the Earth's magnetism show that the magnetic pole is changing its position rapidly; during the past 50 years it has migrated 800 kilometers in Antarctica. About 500 million years ago, the magnetic pole appears to have been in Tonga in the South Pacific. Since the magnetic pole must always be located relatively near the axis of the Earth's rotation, it follows that Antarctica was not then at the bottom of the world as it is today.

Pangaea experienced warm climate during those early Devonian times of 400 million years ago. Organisms included prototypes of modern snails, razor clams over 20 centimeters in length, extinct arthropods about 30 centimeters long, called trilobites, as well as the still extant brachiopod *Lingula* which looks superficially like a scallop. Some of these fossils are within 350 kilometers of the present South Pole. Indications, therefore, are that

Opposite. While continental ice changes little during the course of a year, sea ice, shown here, undergoes striking seasonal variation. Color indicates the age of sea ice. New ice is gray, whereas maturing ice first turns grayish-white, then completely white. At this stage the ice is quite strong, often snow-covered, and ½ to 2 meters thick.

Overleaf. Candle ice lies broken on the cobble shore of Alaska's North Slope. Candle ice forms when ice partially melts and then partially refreezes. The crystalline structure of ice is not especially apparent until the ice begins to melt.

Above. Spread throughout the oceans of the world, diatoms thrive in the cold polar seas. They are the most abundant phytoplankton in the polar oceans. Diatoms are composed of cells enclosed within delicately patterned skeletons of silica. They adhere to the underside of sea ice, turning it brown (top). A close-up shows diatoms aligned on the crystals of ice (bottom).

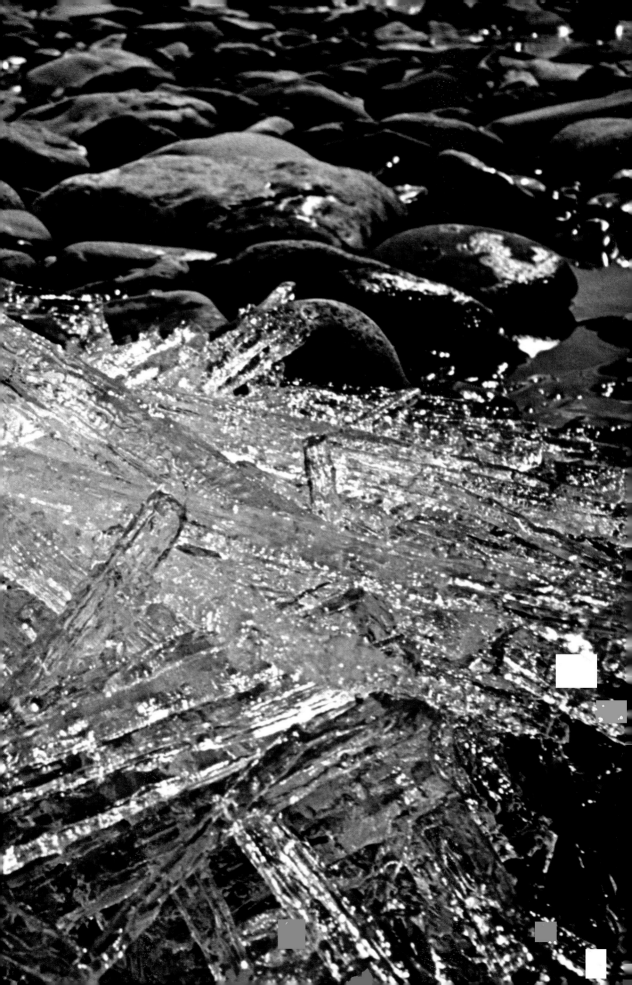

much of present Antarctica was a shallow, warm sea with a sandy to muddy bottom. A little later, during the Carboniferous period, forests existed, which produced the coal beds recently discovered on Antarctica. But, during 50 million years of the late Carboniferous to early Permian periods, the south polar parts of Pangaea bore an ice sheet which grew and shrank many times before it eventually disappeared. This was due to the fact that, by then, what is now South Africa was at the South Pole, surrounded by land that was to become South America, Madagascar, India, Australia, and Antarctica, with what is presently North America and Eurasia at the periphery—all in one gigantic land mass.

Pangaea began to break up about 180 million years ago, during the Triassic period. A northern rift split Pangaea from east to west along a line north of the Equator, creating Laurasia, composed of present day North America and Eurasia, and Gondwanaland, composed of what are now South America, Africa, Australia, India, and Antarctica. As the continents formed and moved apart, they left detached pieces in the form of islands which also drifted apart. The mechanism for this movement of continents over the Earth's surface is described as *plate tectonics* (from a Greek word for a carpenter or builder). These tectonic plates are continental "building blocks." Most continents rest on a single plate. The Arctic is composed of two plates, the North American and Eurasian. Antarctica rests on its own Antarctic Plate. Tectonic plates have boundaries which are seismically very active, exhibiting strong earthquakes and vulcanism. At the boundary in the Antarctic region, southeast of the South American Plate, lies a string of islands on what is called the Scotia Arc. This region is one of the most active tectonic regions of the world and exposes the subantarctic region to periods of strong seismic activity. Similarly, Baffin Bay, in the region between Canada and Greenland, is also very active even though it is well west of the Mid–Atlantic Ridge that separates the North American and Eurasian Plates. Active volcanos of the polar regions include Mt. Erebus of Antarctica, which rises 3,743 meters above Ross Island and presently emits steam, and those on Iceland, an island sitting squarely on the Mid–Atlantic Ridge that is notoriously volcanic. A new island, Surtsey, was created off its shores by vulcanism in 1963.

During Mesozoic times—the Age of Reptiles—when the continents were drifting apart on their tectonic plates, the world climate was warm enough to support abundant plant growth. But as the continents separated, the similarities between northern and southern faunal assemblages decreased. By the early Cenozoic—the Age of Mammals—the continents had assumed their present positions, with Antarctica being situated over the South Pole and the northern continents being jammed together around the isolated Arctic Ocean. And it was only a little later that our present Ice Age began. Some scientists place the beginning of this age as long ago as 40 million years when the Antarctic Ice Sheet began to form. It was not until about 16 million years ago, however, that this ice mass had grown enough in size to cover the continent and reach the shores of Antarctica. The same processes that produced this ice mass also cooled the Earth's oceans by

Opposite. Illuminated by a brilliant October sunset, pack ice stretches into the Southern Ocean. While icebergs are composed of frozen fresh water, pack ice is made of frozen ocean water.

Overleaf. Pancake ice is formed when ice floes, nearing the "front" or open water, collide because of waves or swells. As a result of water movement and collision, these forms are rounded.

Above. Icebergs spawned by the glaciers of Antarctica sail through the frigid sea. Ice floats because it has a lower density than water in a liquid state. Sometimes the melting remains of once-huge Antarctic icebergs last until they have drifted as far north as the subtropical convergence (40° south latitude).

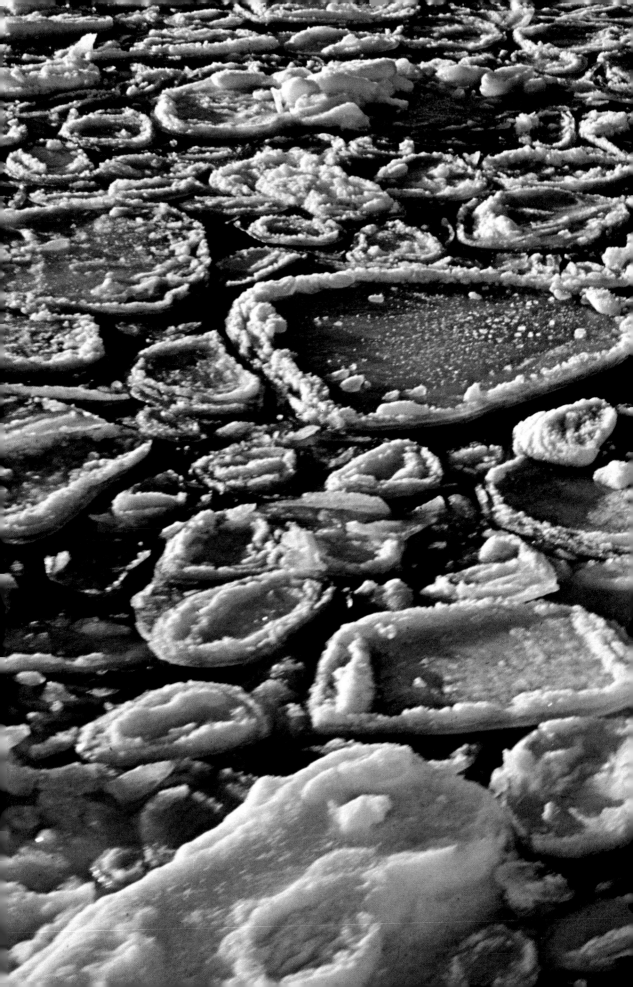

37 top. *The cracking of the tundra soil in Canada's western Arctic, east of the Mackenzie River Delta and near the Beaufort Sea, produces polygonal patterning. This results when water freezes in spaces within the soil and expands as ice. The ice causes the soil to bulge; then, in spring, the ice cracks and melts.*

Center. *Caribou* (Rangifer tarandus) *travel across soil polygons on Alaska's North Slope in June.*

Bottom. *During the summer, pools of water sometimes collect in the tundra's "low center" polygons because soil that is still frozen solid prevents drainage.*

Overleaf. *A slash in the tundra near Noluck Lake in Alaska reveals ice and tundra soil. Below the surface soil, which freezes and thaws seasonally, lies perpetually frozen permafrost, sometimes reaching a depth of 600 meters.*

sending almost freezing ocean waters northward toward the Equator and beyond. This created a new environment for marine life. The accumulating ice mass also lowered sea levels to expose much more land than had been formerly present. Ice masses tie up the Earth's water, leaving less to fill up ocean basins. Partly as a result of lower sea levels induced by the accumulated ice, the Central American isthmus was exposed about 4 million years ago. This separated the tropical Atlantic and Pacific oceans from one another, greatly reducing the amount of warm Atlantic water reaching the Arctic. Thus, an ice sheet began to form over Greenland and then over North America and Eurasia. The Pleistocene Ice Age had begun. It still lasts today.

During the North American Pleistocene, the massive Laurentide Ice Sheet, centered in east-central Canada, extended southward to Ohio and New York and westward to coalesce with the western North American Cordilleran Ice Sheet. This effectively cut off the bulk of southerly flora and fauna from Arctic forms of life. At its maximum, this great ice sheet was about the same size and thickness as that which exists on Antarctica today, or perhaps even a little larger. The Eurasian ice extent was also great but not continuous; corridors existed which allowed living things to move from the Arctic to the south. Together, all the Pleistocene ice sheets—north and south—held so much water that the ocean level was 100 meters lower than it is today, and vast areas of continental shelf were dry lands occupied by terrestrial life. One such exposed shelf area was called Beringia—the land bridge between Asia and North America.

During the Pleistocene, the glaciers alternately advanced and retreated. The last major glaciation is called the Wisconsin in North America and the Würm in Europe. About 20,000 years ago, this glacial period was at its peak; subsequently, the North American and European glacial sheets began to melt. It is fascinating to speculate on this vast melt–down, which raised sea level almost 100 meters over the next 10,000 years. Glacial sheets grow slowly, but they melt more rapidly. One scientist speculates that the Laurentide Ice Sheet might have melted at the rate of 1,500 cubic kilometers of water annually. The Mississippi River, which would have drained much of the ice-covered Laurentide region, would thus have been flooded with up to four times its present annual average volume. During extraordinarily high rainfall and melt–down years, the volume could well have reached twelve times the present average. It is not beyond the imagination to extrapolate from the Mississippi to other rivers draining Ice Age glaciers and to picture northern continental flooding of proportions far beyond anything now known.

This melting—which occurred to a much lesser extent in Antarctica—had great consequences for Arctic life. Although much of the history of Pleistocene life, its evolution and intercontinental migrations, remains vague to this day, it is at least clear that very dramatic changes occurred. During the height of the Wisconsin/Würm, movement from north to south was restricted to a few ice-free corridors in Eurasia. And because of the Beringian Land Bridge which connected Asia to the North American Arctic, Arctic life in North America was really "Asian" in character. As the ice melted, the Beringian Land Bridge

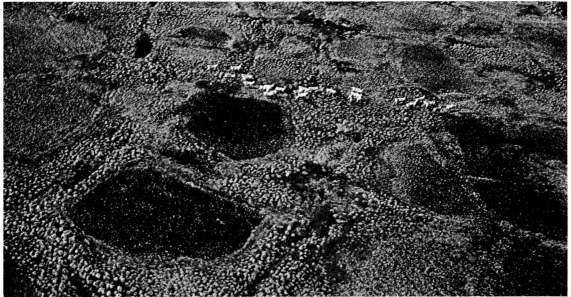

Top. *On Alaska's North Slope, grasses emerge from the snow, which insulates the plants against the cold.*

Bottom. *During the summer, tundra tussocks may grow over a half meter high on Alaska's North Slope. The ice that melts on the surface cannot penetrate very far into the soil because of solidly frozen permafrost below. The water therefore collects on and near the surface, turning the ground into a quagmire.*

was submerged, cutting off the connection between Asian and North American lands; the glacier-free corridors between the Arctic and the south became even wider. Arctic species spread ever more widely through the now ice-free areas of the Arctic region and warmer-living invaders from the south moved north to share the same habitats. Many species became extinct, such as mammoths, mastodons, wooly rhinoceroses, and others. The Arctic region became newly populated by a mixture of Arctic species which managed to survive, and by more southerly ranging species.

Some strictly Arctic mammals that do not range southward are the polar bear, Arctic hare, Arctic fox, collared lemming, bowhead whale, and the ice-inhabiting seals and walrus. Of these, the polar bear and Arctic fox are the prime examples of species which range over the whole extent of the Arctic regions, both land and sea. Examples of species that occupy Arctic areas, but also range southward are the brown lemming, brown bear, lynx, wolf, wolverine, and many creatures that migrate with the seasons, such as the gray whale, fur seal, and many birds. Of course, things are not quite so simple. As the glaciers expanded, some species became trapped in protected pockets called refugia; then, as the glaciers receded, such species were either left behind or expanded to repopulate former habitats, depending upon their adaptive and competitive abilities. Examples of Arctic-like refugia exist in high alpine zones where such animals as marmots, pikas, ravens, and snowshoe hares are found far south of areas where they would be expected to live on the basis of latitude alone.

In the Antarctic, its encircling Southern Ocean largely restricts the ranges of most aquatic species that compose its rich living communities. Into this region venture a few species such as the great whales on annual migrations, but many of its oceanic species—and some continental ones too—are just as isolated as they have been since Antarctica's breakaway from the other continents millions of years ago. Furthermore, it appears that the Arctic region's climate fluctuates more markedly than that of the Antarctic. Plant remains from about 5,000 years ago indicate that much of the Arctic was warmer than it is today. Are we to experience another major continental glaciation? No one can tell.

Challenge of the Polar Regions

Perhaps the general impression has been, for most people, that the polar regions are monotonous lands and seas of icy cold. True, the Antarctic and Greenland ice sheets are among the most forbidding places on Earth, having almost no life; much of the polar regions receive very little precipitation and are desert-like in their dryness. But the polar regions do have their own particular variety. Biomes are the major characteristic animal and plant associations of our planet. Thus, we may speak of a tundra biome, an oceanic biome, a coastal and benthic biome, and so forth. These associations closely follow the climatic and physiographic features spoken of above.

Most life of the Antarctic region is clearly sea-dominated. There is no expansive tundra of the kind that dominates the Arctic's landscape. But there are lichens, grasses, and mosses that support animal life. And strange anomalies

occur which continue to fascinate scientists—the dry
valleys near the Ross Sea and the ice-free blue and green
lakes of eastern Antarctica, for example. Antarctica is
divided into a larger eastern and a smaller western
portion, separated by a high mountain range. Gigantic ice
shelves—up to over 700 meters thick at the continental
border and 250 meters thick at their outer extremities—
calve off huge tabular icebergs which often contain over
100 square kilometers of ice.

The setting for life in the Antarctic region is in sharp
contrast to the Arctic region's vast expanses of tundra and
to its sea, where icebergs, calved mostly from the glaciers
of west Greenland and Ellesmere, are of only relatively
minute proportions. But the thing to remember is that
every individual animal and plant lives not in a global
climate, but in a microclimate all its own. Lemmings
burrow beneath an insulating mantle of snow and tundra
vegetation, there to remain fully awake and quite cozy
through the winter. In contrast, the much larger bears
den up for a winter's sleep. The interiors of Siberia and
Antarctica are stupefyingly cold, but along their coasts
and offshore islands the temperature may not be lower
than −15° C during the winter; the sea has a warming
effect.

Temperature is a deceptive yardstick. As scientists well
know, air temperature may be low, but radiation from the
sun, the chill of wind, and the relative humidity must be
considered to calculate the true temperature which affects
life. Seemingly small matters, such as the slope of the
landscape, may also make great differences because of the
low angle of the sun in polar regions. These and other
factors alter the seemingly uniformly cold environment
into a mosaic of microclimates much more varied than one
might expect.

Polar winters are long, lasting one-half to two-thirds of
every year. Spring and fall are sudden and short, lasting
only a month or two each. That leaves summer with but 2
to 3 months. Those species that have adapted to the polar
regions have done so by means of whole arrays of
exquisite adaptations, as we shall see in the chapters that
follow. Such adaptations are the result of the challenge to
life in the polar regions.

Those of us who explore these regions know how few are
man's physiological adaptations to the cold. Through the
development of clothing and other adaptations, man has
been able to inhabit the Arctic. However, the ice of the
Southern Ocean and the distance of Antarctica from other
continents have prevented man from inhabiting the
continent until the turn of the twentieth century; that has
been left to modern scientists and explorers. Uppermost
in one's mind, however, is how precisely wildlife is keyed
to seasonal climactic fluctuations in the polar regions. In
these regions, more than anywhere else on Earth, the
timing of events is the key to survival—for man and
wildlife alike.

*Overleaf. Pingos, such as this one
along the Mackenzie River in
Canada, are caused by frost
heaves within the soil. Pingos
may stand 30 meters high and
remain for years.*

41

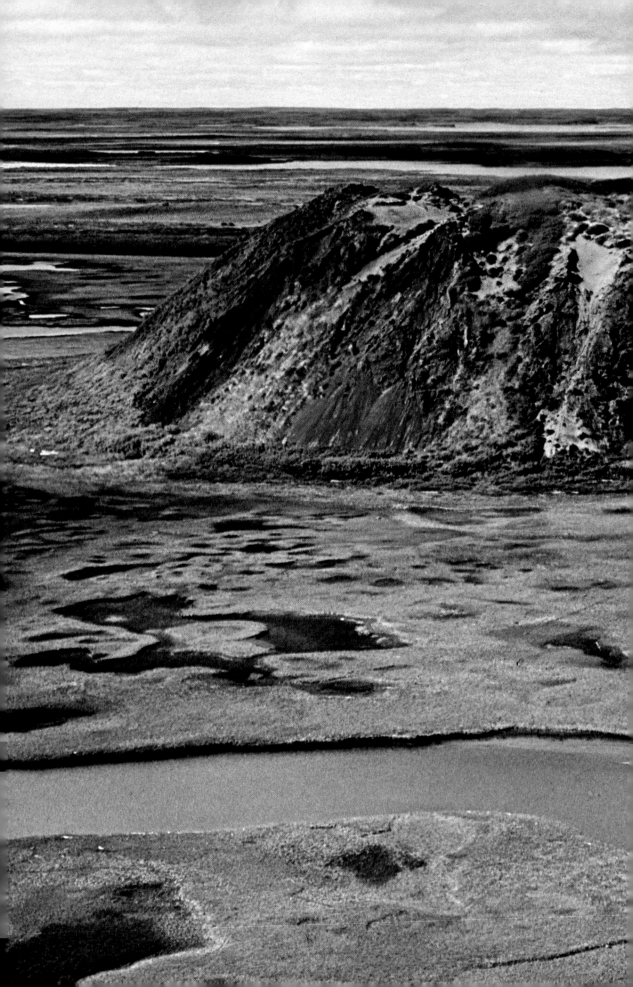

Survival in a Cold Climate

Some polar wildlife species are year-round residents; some are seasonal visitors. Some live on a critical edge of survival, and others can live only in their polar habitat. All have one thing in common—they are adapted for polar life. That is, they have attributes that are suited to both the physical and biological environment and to the many stresses that are imposed in the polar climate. Furthermore, they have acquired those properties through evolutionary processes that have paralleled the changes of the Ice Age in which we are still presently immersed.

There can be no weak links in the chain of evolutionary adaptation, or extinction must certainly follow. Each species must obtain food, find shelter, reproduce, interact with its neighbors, and regulate its internal physiological mechanisms. Adaptive strategies include anatomical adaptations such as body size and shape, insulation such as fur and blubber, heat-dissipating mechanisms such as flippers and flukes and ears, and large feet for walking on snow. They include physiological mechanisms such as enzymes which perform optimally at low temperatures, antifreezes in blood, and even a total lack of hemoglobin and red blood cells in one whole family of Antarctic fishes. And they include behavior which, remarkably in some cases, allows survival in polar regions in spite of apparent lack of anatomical and physiological fitness. A newborn walrus could not survive on ice without the "brooding" shelter of its mother. Lemmings could not survive if they did not store plant material under the insulative layer of snow that covers their tundra home in winter. Baleen whales travel to polar regions in summer to take advantage of the rich plankton available to them at that time; an exception is the Arctic bowhead whale which, like the polar seals and walrus, has become permanently adapted to a habitat of sea ice.

The polar regions, it would appear, "filter out" species from elsewhere that would invade them. That is, the more polar the fewer species—those from more temperate places most often cannot meet the harsh environmental stresses of polar regions. However, many do make it. And those that do have adapted so well that some can live nowhere else. In some cases, the process of evolutionary adaptation has produced some remarkable parallelisms and convergences in the polar regions. At these two ends of the Earth are found look-alikes which may or may not be closely related. Parallel lines of evolution, where rather closely related species evolve similar life history strategies are exemplified by the ice-inhabiting seals. In contrast, the Antarctic penguins and Arctic look-alikes, the auks and their relatives, have converged; they are hardly related at all, but live similar lives.

Consider the fishes. The Arctic region has no endemic family of fishes—that is, no family not found anywhere else. In the Southern Ocean, the opposite is nearly true. About 120 fish species occur there, and 90 percent of them are endemic. The Notothenioidea (there is no accepted vernacular name for this order, partly because there have been no fishermen in Antarctica to name them) represent 75 percent of all continental shelf species. The presence of such a large group and its numerous species reflects that ocean's long isolation from other oceans.

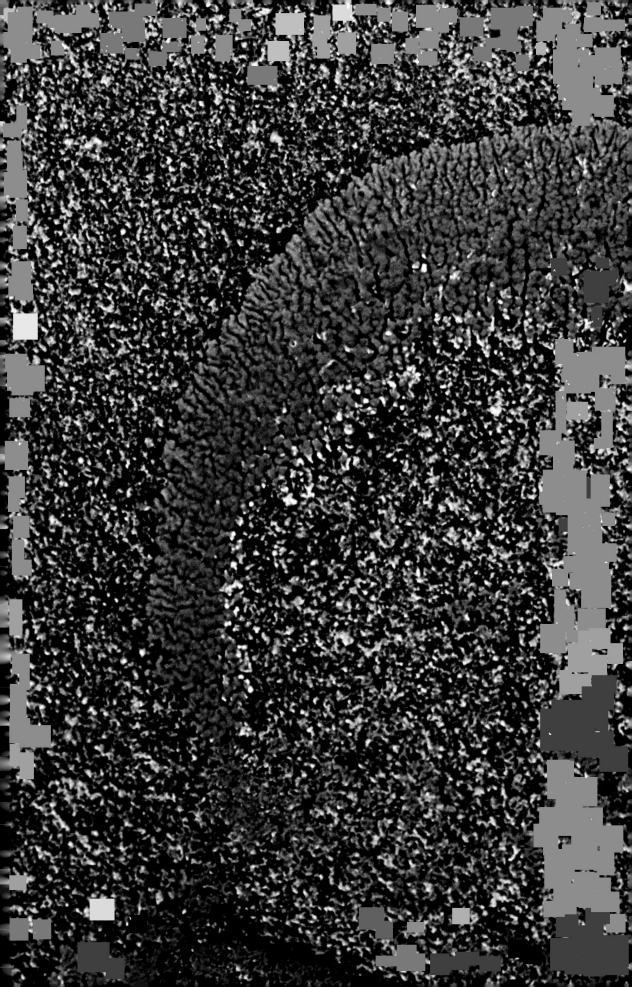

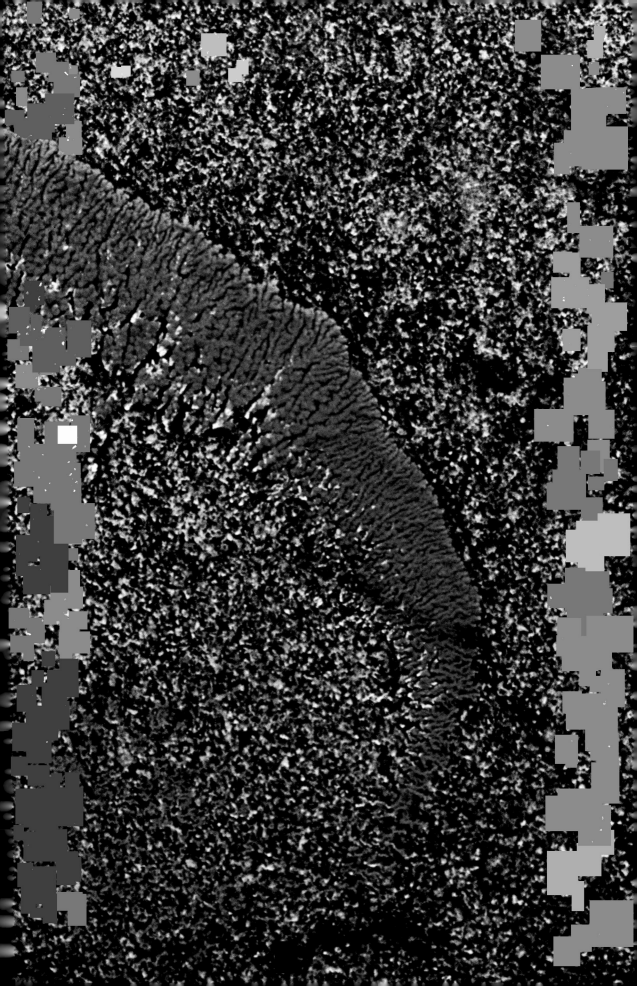

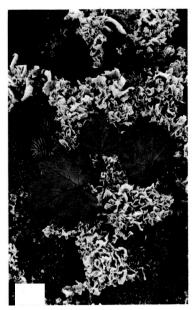

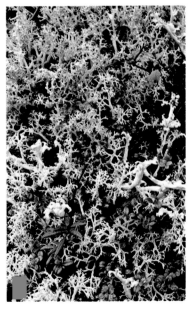

Top. *A lichen (probably* Centraria islandica) *grows on the tundra. Although lichens flourish in some of the Earth's most hostile natural environments, they cannot withstand air pollution. These unusual plants are rare in heavily industrialized areas.*

Bottom. *Vast areas of the Arctic tundra are carpeted with a lichen called "reindeer moss"* (Cladonia rangifera). *As its name suggests, this plant is important as food to reindeer, called "caribou" in North America.*

The evolution of these notothenioids has produced forms which closely resemble far-removed families of fishes, a remarkable case of convergent evolution—that is, the evolution of look-alikes from different origins. For example, the so-called Antarctic cod family (Notothenidae) contains species that are much like the greenlings and cods of the Northern Hemisphere. Among them is the giant Antarctic cod (*Dissostichus mawsoni*), largest of all Antarctic fishes; it is 1½ meters long and weighs 50 to 70 kilograms. Occasionally, Weddell seals have been known to bring these giant fish to the ice surface and consume them at their leisure. Other notothenids are much smaller, including the very cold-adapted *Trematomus bernacchii*, which lives under landfast ice. One genus of this family, *Pleurogramma*, includes the Antarctic herring, the only truly pelagic, plankton-eating Antarctic fish. The plunder fishes (Harpagiferidae) are like northern sculpins, usually bearing a long barbel on the lower jaw. The dragon fishes (Bathydraconidae) are elongated and superficially resemble pikes, but unlike pikes, they mostly rest on the bottom. And the most unusual of all, the white-blooded fishes (Channichthyidae) have no red blood cells and no hemoglobin. They are large and predatory and also look something like pikes.

The Antarctic fishes are an example of the confusion that arises when one hears that polar region life lacks diversity. Surely, there are fewer total species than in temperate regions or the tropics, but where else may one see such a bounty of whales, seals, auks, penguins, and notothenioids? Many of the groups of animals that have evolved here live nowhere else.

An Extreme of Adaptation

The white-blooded icefish (*Pagetopsis macropterus*) of the Southern Ocean swims near the bottom and comes to rest on some convenient platform such as the top of a sponge. At half-minute intervals it moves, but not very far, covering 2 to 3 meters a minute by rowing motions of its wing-like pectoral fins. If it is captured and released in water a few meters above the bottom, it may swim for a minute, but then it sinks slowly to the bottom. If threatened by a diver, it opens its mouth wide, spreads its gill covers, erects the dorsal fin, flares its pectorals, and holds its body in a curve—evidently presenting a more formidable appearance in the face of danger. It certainly cannot escape by speed. The icefish cannot afford too great an expenditure of energy, for it has no red blood cells to carry oxygen to its tissues.

All vertebrates, except the majority of Antarctic icefishes of the family Channichthyidae, have red blood cells. More specifically, some icefishes have up to 30 percent of the solid materials of their blood as red blood cells, compared with 95 to 99 percent in most vertebrates; most have no red blood cells and, therefore, no hemoglobin at all. Only in such permanently frigid waters as those of the Southern Ocean is such absence possible; the colder the water, the more oxygen it can contain. It appears that the notothenioid fishes have a tendency toward a low red blood cell count; one might say that they are anemic. They compensate for this in a number of ways, most obviously through reduced activity. Recent research has also shown that they have a larger blood volume, higher heart output, and a higher rate of blood flow than other fishes. And they have a great many capillaries in their skin and fins by means of which oxygen is extracted from the water. Many years of evolution evidently were required to produce such extraordinary adaptations as red-bloodlessness. It is by no means clear, in fact, what the ultimate advantage is. There is less need for red blood cells in the oxygen-rich waters of the Southern Ocean, but the absence of red blood cells means living a more sedentary life. In the Arctic, a fish cannot live without red blood cells. There the fish fauna is dominated by species from north temperate waters, such as herrings, cods, salmons, whitefishes, and halibuts, which have invaded the Arctic. The shelf waters and rivers of the Arctic warm to 10°C or more at the surface in summer and fishes must be able to adapt to such high temperatures, the adaptations including retention of their normal red blood cell count. The Pacific herring (*Clupea pallasi*) is really a fish of the temperate zone but it breeds all the way into the Arctic. It spawns inshore and each female's 20,000 eggs hatch most successfully if attached to vegetation where good circulation surrounds the eggs. Similarly, the Arctic cod (*Boreogadus saida*) is found on all shelves adjacent to the Arctic Basin. Like the herring, it spawns in inshore waters. Millions of these fish may school unpredictably in bays and lagoons. Both the herring and the cod are important food for seals and whales, and form vital links between zooplankton and marine mammals in the Arctic food web.

Living Together

The animals and plants that occur and interact together in a particular place, be it lake, tundra, or sea, constitute a community. They interact, of course, in many ways. Some species are symbiotic, and depend upon one another to mutual benefit; a tundra lichen is not one plant, but two, an alga and a fungus living together. Often this symbiosis takes the form of parasitism in which one of the pair benefits and the other may suffer. Most species are not so intimately involved; another way to conceive of community relationships is through a food web. Previously, this was considered to be a chain of who eats whom and is eaten by whom. Thus, various trophic levels may be conceived—the photosynthetic producers at level one; the herbivorous consumers at level two, the carnivorous consumers at level three, and the decomposers, which return basic nutrients from all levels back to level one. Classic food chain examples are reindeer "moss" (*Cladonia*)—actually a lichen—to caribou to wolf; or, phytoplankton to krill to blue whale. Furthermore, these levels may comprise progressively less total weight of organisms, called biomass, in their community. A rule of thumb is that about 80 to 90 percent of biomass is lost from the first to the second level and again from the second to the third. If there were one kilogram on level one, there would be 100 to 200 grams on level two and 10 to 20 on level three. That is, if one were to weigh all materials on the tundra, living or dead—forest plants, animals, insects, and the like—the greatest weight would be in living plants and dead plant matter, and the least in predators. Benthic communities are like terrestrial ones

44. Covering rocks on King George Island in the Antarctic, lichens (Ramalia and Xanthoria) live where few other plants are able to survive. The lichen is not one plant but two—a partnership of an alga and a fungus. The fungus has unusually tough threads that anchor the lichen to rock or soil and bind together the many minuscule, individual alga plants.

46–47. A lichen (probably Xanthoria elegans) forms a delicate pattern on a rock on Somerset Island in the Canadian high Arctic. The fungus threads of the lichen produce acids that eat away at rock, enabling the organism to obtain minerals. The threads also absorb water, which is used by the alga in photosynthesis.

to a degree—especially ones in shallow water where light is intensive enough for photosynthesis. But oceanic communities have fundamental differences from terrestrial and benthic ones. In pelagic polar seas there are no counterparts to the rooted plants that occur on land or to the kelp that occurs near shore in other seas. Plants on land or shore may live for years and often tie up nutrients, such as carbon, in their tissues. Woody plants, for example, have been termed the "bottleneck of ecosystems" because the cellulose forming the wood of the plants may take many years to decompose and release its nutrients.

In the sea, the process of nutrient release and recycling are very different. If one were to weigh all the living materials in the sea's community, the microscopic animals called zooplankton that feed on plants would weigh the most, more even than the phytoplankton or the whales and seals. The plants make up for lack of biomass by their great productivity, reproducing so fast that over a whole year their weight must be many times that of the zooplankton. But at any given time they are not so weighty. This feature in the sea is reflected in the inverted pyramid of biomass. The huge biomass of some Arctic copepods and Antarctic krill is greater than that of their plant food.

But, of course, matters are not as simple as food chains and pyramids suggest, in which each species fits a trophic level neatly. Some species, such as the blue whale, are very obligate feeders, eating only zooplankton. But brown bears may eat berries, fishes, birds, and moose. Each animal has a number of food choices and these choices change with the season and the stage of their development. And as individuals from each level die, they may be eaten by scavengers or be decomposed. However, decomposition is slow in polar regions. Bodies of dead organisms may be eaten before being decomposed; the polar regions have a number of necrophagous animals. Feces decompose slowly too, and may be eaten by copraphagous animals. So it is best not to think in the straight lines of food chains, but in terms of a food web. The trophic levels still exist and so do the pyramids of biomass, but species do not always neatly fit into niches. In fact, it is sometimes hazardous to become too specialized.

Enormous amounts of food are required by some species of polar communities. On the Arctic tundra, the caribou lives on a diet of low plants such as reindeer moss. Every day, on the average, each caribou needs 2 to 3 kilograms of food. A hundred thousand caribou, weighing a total of about 10 million kilograms needs about 200 to 300 tons of tundra plants, almost all of which must be produced in summer. Tundra is not very productive per square kilometer, and this requires caribou herds to wander vast Arctic territories to sustain themselves. Thus, it is mainly the size of the range that gives stability to caribou populations. Disruptions in this continuity are bound to have serious consequences for caribou population size. Oceanic examples are even more spectacular. Walruses may weigh an average of a ton each, taking all sizes into account. There are surely at least 150,000 tons of walrus in those northern waters over the land bridge between Asia and the Americas called Beringia. There, the herds

Opposite. The willow ptarmigan inhabits much of the Arctic. During the summer, its plumage is a mottled reddish-brown, but in the winter it is white, except for black tail, eyes, and bill.

Overleaf. A giant petrel (Macronectes giganteus) *tends its chick on King George Island in the Antarctic. This bird ranges farther into the Southern Ocean— reaching far southern Antarctic shores—than any other member of its family.*

Above. Similar in appearance to the willow ptarmigan (Lagopus lagopus), *the rock ptarmigan* (L. mutus) *lives on rocky mountain slopes throughout most of the Arctic. During the most severe winter weather, its feet sprout a cushion of feathers that serve as snowshoes.*

Top. *The spiderplant* (Saxifraga flagellaris) *of the Arctic tundra produces new plants by sending out runners through which the offspring are nourished by the mother plant. After the new plants have rooted, the runners disintegrate.*

Bottom. *An Arctic marigold* (Caltha palustris *var.* arctica) *blooms in a natural oil seep near the Sagavanirktok River, Alaska. A member of the buttercup family, this plant is adapted to marshy areas in cold climates.*

find access to the water and to a rich food supply of benthic invertebrates only 50 to 150 meters down. In apparent unison among its individuals, each herd feeds and rests, during intensive periods of 36 to 48 hours for each activity. During feeding, each adult weighing 1 to 2 tons may consume about 5 percent of its body weight each day in clams—40 to 80 kilograms or as many as several hundred to a few thousand clams for each animal. Feeding in almost complete darkness at this depth, the walruses root in the bottom with their muzzles much like pigs, and suck the clams out of their shells with a powerful action of the tongue. Contrary to popular tales, they do not use their tusks to dig clams. Feeding must be intensive for the females particularly. It is therefore essential that they accumulate a heavy supply of fat, for pregnant or nursing mammals require much more energy than at any other time of their lives. Each day the Bering and Chukchi Seas must provide 7,500 tons of walrus food —and that's a lot of clams. Walruses roam wide and far to find such supplies. Man is increasingly competing for this supply, but to overfish this area would be to threaten the walrus' food supply.

Polar Ecosystems
Near colonies of seabirds, such as penguins, vegetation is usually sparse. On some Antarctic islands where seals and seabirds join the penguins, the soil is rank with excreta in such quantities that it is toxic to vegetation. The soils there contain large amounts of phosphorous and inorganic nitrogen which the melting snow and ice and the fall of summer rain leach away to nourish nearby waters. This provides a dramatic example of nutrient cycling: penguins and seals feed in the sea, come on land and provide nutrients in the form of feces to terrestrial organisms, and go to the sea again to feed. This illustrates a dimension beyond the living community to the ecosystem.

Scientists have coined the term "ecosystem" to express the fundamental functional unit of nature. It comprises all the animals and plants and the inorganic materials within an area. It is, as one scientist puts it, an internally coherent system of interrelated processes within physical boundaries. The concept of the ecosystem can be analogously described by looking at the human body with its independent parts such as arms, legs, eyes, and ears; each serves different functions, but depends on an integrated system of physiological processes which coordinates them. These processes provide nourishment for growth and take away waste products. In sum, they keep the body functioning properly. Ecosystems also have identifiable parts—species, water, ice, chemicals, substrate, etc.—all coordinated by certain ecological processes that supply nutrients and take waste away, or convert waste into some useable form. The boundaries that define an ecosystem, unlike those of the human body, are difficult to identify, as ecosystems are constantly changing with environmental variables. Some are small— thaw-melt tundra ponds—and some are large—the entire pelagic Southern Ocean.

Ecosystems have been defined as energy-processing units whereby nutrients and other materials are used and cycled in efficient and predictable ways. The energy

A groundsel (Senecio pseudoaranca) *buds* (top) *and blooms* (bottom) *on the Arctic tundra. During the short spring and summer, tundra flowers bloom profusely, though briefly. Groundsels favor open country and usually live in soils—such as those of the Arctic—not rich enough to support really lush vegetation.*

Above. *Backed by the Larsen Ice Shelf and the Weddell Sea, the Antarctic Peninsula reaches out from the mainland toward the tip of South America. The red lichen* (Caloplaca), *one of the 350 different kinds of lichens in Antarctica, could not exist on this rocky terrain were it not for birds roosting nearby. The nitrogen from the birds' droppings fertilizes this lichen.*

Right. *Growing out of a rock cleft on the Antarctic Peninsula, this grass,* Deschampsia antarctica, *is one of two species of flowering plants native to the continent. Both species are restricted to the peninsula; only here are conditions mild enough for plants other than lichens and mosses.*

Overleaf. *The snow-white coat of an Arctic hare (Lepus arcticus) stands out against the summer vegetation on Bathurst Island, in the far north of the Canadian Arctic. A bit further south, this species darkens in summer, but in the high Arctic it remains white year-round.*

supplied by the sun is, thus, captured by photosynthesis to produce plant material. Consumers shuffle the nutrients through food webs and trophic levels, producing waste products, and all of those processes may be understood together only in the context of ecosystems. Also, ecosystems may largely be characterized by how they store and recycle materials. Some ecosystems are fast and some are slow, largely a reflection of how fast decomposition and recycling of nutrients and other materials occur. There are many factors affecting production, consumption, decomposition, and recycling: soil acidity, temperatures, moisture, light, wind, currents, and energy supply, to name a few. The dynamics of ecosystems is no doubt the most complex of topics. To trace out all ecosystem relationships would produce a wiring diagram that would put the most advanced computer to shame. Yet some of the connections are dominant and it is upon those that ecosystem ecologists concentrate.

Production in a Frozen Sea
As we have seen, sea ice varies greatly in extent from winter to summer. Sea ice begins to form at about −2°C. A process of great beauty, it begins when a thin surface film of tiny ice crystals, called grease ice, appears. Soon a layer of thin gray ice, thin enough to allow us to see the dark water beneath it, consolidates. This veneer may be broken into fragments by wind and wave, producing geometric designs, but it reforms and soon thickens sufficiently for a person to walk on it—or for a seal to haul out to rest on it. At this stage, the ice layer may be about 15 to 25 centimeters thick, but such dimensions are difficult to state precisely because sea ice is not as solid as freshwater ice, having small pockets of brine. When sea ice does thicken to gray-white ice and then to white ice, it is quite strong, often snow-covered, and ½ to 2 meters thick. By that time, the ice cover of the sea is extensive enough to be called pack ice. The entire pack is ever on the move; a rate of 10 kilometers a day is not rare, but the usual speed is about ½ to 5 kilometers. The maximum recorded speed is near 60 kilometers.
The pack ice cover is not uniform over the sea. It is molded and shaped by wind and current and broken into irregular floes and may be pounded into round pancake ice near the front where the pack meets the open sea. Melting and evaporation occur at its surface, while on the underside delicate crystals sometimes accumulate into stalactite-like projections over a meter long. Like crystal chandeliers, these transmit light into the subice water.
Winds, especially, deform the entire pack, producing river-like leads and lake-like polynyas where masses of ice diverge. Where ice masses converge, hummocks and ridges are thrust upward. Sheet-like chunks pile up, and may reach many meters below the surface. Ice which does not melt in summer may become the base for the formation of hard, thick multiyear ice—an uncommon condition in the Antarctic but one that forms the major portion of sea ice over the Arctic Ocean Basin.
The sea ice, far from being inhospitable to life, as is generally assumed, is quite beneficial in at least two ways. First, the delicate crystalline underside of the ice has

many interstices that are inhabited by entire communities of life—protozoans, small crustaceans, and worms, among others. The most important of these inhabitants are plants called diatoms, which form vital nutrition for the food webs of these seas. Second, sea ice, being solid enough to bear the weight of polar bears, seals, and walruses, has allowed such animals to extend their ranges far out to sea. Using such sea ice, many species may even live at sea permanently; seals, for example, must bear their young on solid surfaces, yet must feed at sea. The sea ice is a "land" far from land for them, and some of them now never come ashore. Furthermore, polar bears and their camp followers, the Arctic foxes, would be less able to prey on seals without sea ice on which to move about. Without understanding the value of this icy component of the polar ocean environment, one cannot comprehend polar ocean life. The whole ecosystem of the polar seas would be far different without it.

Looking more closely at the diatoms, we find that these brownish, microscopic plants with beautiful siliceous skeletons, coat virtually the entire subsurface of sea ice at certain times of the year. Diatoms are able to maintain vigorous growth at very low light levels—less than a hundredth of the light at the upper surface of the ice. This is an important function within ice-covered seas. Critical light levels for diatom growth are reached in the polar regions from late winter to early spring, depending on the latitude. The diatom layer becomes so dense that it seriously reduces the light in the water below it, preventing photosynthesis there. The diatoms, therefore, engage in the only significant photosynthesis in the ice-covered sea during the winter and spring. It is difficult to estimate the amount of diatoms in the polar seas, but there is no doubt that it is great and very important. This inverted benthos extracts nutrients from the sea and provides the food for many invertebrates that graze on it; these, in turn are food for fishes, seals, and others. Here, then, is a highly effective mechanism which extends the growing period significantly at latitudes where the season for growth would otherwise be very short. In some locations, there is a second, falltime period of diatom growth, but this cannot be so significant as the one in the springtime.

When the sea ice begins to break up and melt in late spring and early summer, the diatoms stop growing on the underside of the ice. In summer in ice-free water, a "summer bloom" may become the major producer of life in the polar seas, as in all other seas. Evidently this bloom is lacking in the inshore waters of the Arctic's Bering and Chukchi Seas. There, the subice diatoms fall to the bottom in early summer, leaving the surface waters stripped of nutrients. This subice source of primary production is vital and millions of hungry animals depend upon it, directly or indirectly.

Research tells us that sea ice, with brine pockets on its underside, can be extraordinarily rich in nutrients and offers stable living conditions for certain forms of life. Some species may even depend upon sea ice for wintering over. And it appears likely that sea ice and microscopic algae interact in such a way that the algae may influence the form of the sea ice itself. Diatoms incorporated into near-surface ice layers darken the sea ice, and the

Looking almost elfish, an Arctic hare stands up on its hind legs for a look across the bleak landscape of Bathurst Island. This animal can also run on its hind legs.

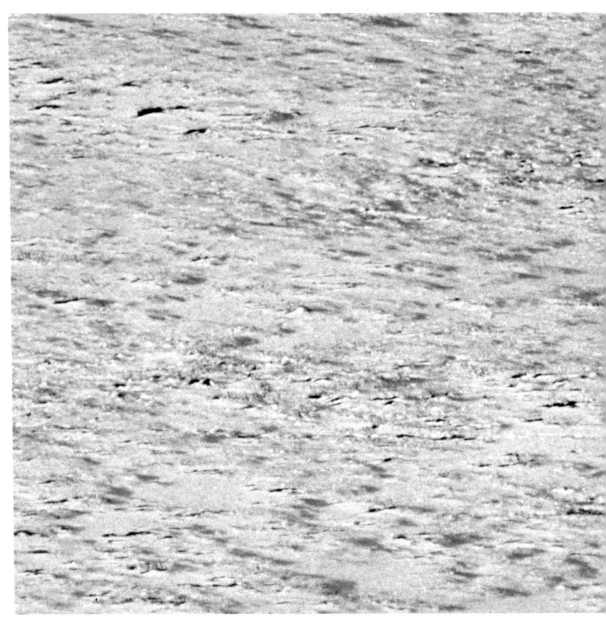

Above. *Near the northern Hudson Bay area, male polar bears* (Ursus maritimus) *spar, a usual practice during the mating season. The polar bear is marvelously adapted to life in the Arctic. Its fur is so thick that little water reaches the bear's skin.*

Left. *Using its mother for a pillow, a polar bear cub dozes along the Hudson Bay coast. Youngsters are born during the winter in dens on land or shorefast ice. The snow cover insulates the den, keeping the mother—and the young—warm. The female polar bear usually has two cubs per breeding season, and since the young stay with her for almost 2 years, she does not mate annually, but only after she is free of her progeny.*

Overleaf. *A colony of king penguins* (Aptenodytes patagonicus) *gathers to breed on a subantarctic island. Most penguins breed at the same location year after year. Among the advantages derived from colonial breeding are safety and warmth: There are many eyes to watch for predators, and when it is very cold the penguins huddle together, sharing body heat.*

capacity of ice to reflect light, called albedo, also changes. This can cause large-scale changes in the absorption of solar energy over extensive areas of ice since it greatly accelerates the formation of melt pools in summer and may affect formation of leads and polynyas in winter by weakening certain ice areas. These leads and polynyas affect the warming of water by solar radiation and provide open areas where the seals, walruses, and penguins of polar seas may haul out to rest or enter the water to feed. The possibility that sea ice diatoms facilitate lead and polynya formation and thus extend their benefits beyond nutrition has yet to be explored.

Finding Food and Direction Under Ice
It is not sufficient only to consider production mechanisms. If food is to be consumed, animals must also find it. Questions of food-finding and underwater navigation are only partially answered.

Vision is of limited use under water because of water's limited clarity compared to air; thus, sound is an important way for some species to find food, identify objects, and navigate in the sea. They do this by means of echolocation—sounds produced by an animal strike an object and are reflected back to the animal, telling it what lies ahead. Ships use the same method, called sonar, to detect and locate submarines or schools of fish. Bats, which often fly in the dark, were the first animals known to use echolocation to find their flying insect prey. Now several species of porpoises are known to have this ability, but no seal or sea lion has yet been shown to use it.

Underwater observations of marine mammals are so difficult that many questions remain unanswered. How do marine mammals find their food in the depths to which they dive? How do they relocate their diving holes in the ice through which they must emerge to breathe? And how does a seal locate its pup on moving sea ice where it may have been left hours before?

To the first of these questions, it has been suggested that these mammals have much more acute vision at very low light levels than do humans. But experiments with seals throw doubt on this. It also seems unsatisfactory to explain the Weddell seal's ability to find food at a depth of 600 meters or more, particularly when the water is under 2 meters of ice where light is already reduced to a hundredth of its surface intensity.

To the question of how a Weddell or ring seal finds its way back to a hole or den in the ice, particularly when that hole or den can only be clearly seen from directly below, a plausible answer might be that the seal memorizes bottom topography or knows an area much as we memorize city streets. Or perhaps it can hear its fellows in the colony above. Still, there are no ready answers.

But the most baffling question is, how does a spotted seal (*Phoca largha*) of Beringia find its pup on moving ice? This is a solitary species which, unlike the walrus, the crabeater, harp seal, or other gregarious species, cannot depend upon communication with its fellows as an aid to finding its way back to a herd. The female bears the pup on moving pancake ice near the sea ice front which may be moving at several kilometers a day. She is largely alone with her pup until joined by a male when she is sexually receptive—near the completion of the 4 to 6 week nursing period. Further, the ice is not only moving as a whole, but individual pans are constantly changing position relative to one another. There are apparently very few landmarks for this seal to remember in this ever-shifting scene. There is also little likelihood that a swimming seal can see its young on top of the ice above it. To make matters more difficult, this is the time of greatest subice diatom production, with the murky water limiting visibility to 2 to 3 meters. Can the female smell traces of her pup? Does she possess an inertial navigation system, a built-in ability to know the direction of the pup which she has left? Perhaps the female seems to disappear, but is not far out of sight of the ice on which her pup lies. The answer still eludes us.

Time and Timing of Events
The blooming of diatoms dramatically illustrates a major feature of polar regions—their strong seasonality. Not only are reproduction seasons short; they also occur suddenly. Spring hardly seems to occur some years in the tundra. All of a sudden, frozen rivers break their icy bonds, and the snow disappears in a few short weeks to be replaced by a burst of flowers.

The study of time and timing of events is called phenology. One cannot understand the polar regions without considering it in detail. For instance, should animals not reproduce early enough, their young would miss the growth of plants or insects which nourish them. This "start up" time is essential; the whole food web depends on it. A clue to just how suddenly spring occurs lies in day length. Each spring month, day length increases almost four hours at the Arctic and Antarctic Circles, compared with half that time at the Tropics of Cancer and Capricorn. This means that the rate of warming is correspondingly rapid. By the first day of summer, the longest day of the year, polar regions are receiving more light energy a day than the tropics. Animals and plants respond precisely to these seasonal changes. When days are sufficiently warm, sudden swarms of biting insects take their blood meals on cue so that their eggs may hatch into larvae in time to feed on the rich planktonic soups of tundra ponds before they freeze in fall.

With equal precision, the tundra-breeding birds and pond-breeding waterfowl arrive to lay eggs and raise chicks to flight size before the freeze shuts the ecosystem down into winter dormancy—or at least into periods of vastly reduced activity. The ever active lemmings and beavers store enough plant matter near their protected winter homes to supplement their winter grazing. Some years, of course, prove more hazardous. Birds migrate as a response to lengthening days, but vagaries of weather at their destination may pose serious problems. On the morning after a not unusual snowfall in late spring or early summer, some birds may be seen perched miserably, their nests covered. Penguins may become utterly drifted in and may suffer many casualties. But mostly, long years of adaptation have meant that animals correctly judge the seasons. And, their physiological and behavioral mechanisms allow them to tolerate its vicissitudes.

A most dramatic case in point is the reproduction and

Above. *A south polar skua* (Catharacta maccormicki) *flies over three emperor penguin chicks* (Aptenodytes forsteri). *The skua preys on penguin eggs and chicks, but it usually does not attack adult birds.*

Overleaf. *In the Falkland Islands, a skua* (Catharacta lonnbergi) *grabs and kills a gentoo penguin chick* (Pygnoscelis papua).

Second overleaf. *Red algae* (Chlamydomas nivalis) *from the sea stain the snow at Paradise Bay in the Antarctic. Although this alga contains chlorophyll, its green color is masked in winter by a pinkish-red pigment that may protect it from the sun's radiation.*

Arctic ground squirrels (Spermophilus undulatus) *live throughout the Arctic and subarctic, mostly on the mainland, but also on islands off Alaska. They inhabit tundra and meadows, hibernating in winter for 7 months and feeding in warm weather on plants and small invertebrates.*

growth of the young of ice-inhabiting seals. Each year while the ice is still stable, the species which inhabit shorefast ice—the Southern Ocean Weddell seal (*Leptonychotes weddelli*) and the Arctic ringed seal (*Phoca hispida*)—bear young in a stable sea ice habitat. Their young are fast growing, tripling their weight in 4 to 6 weeks of nursing. They must be weaned shortly after birth lest their sea ice home break up before they have accumulated enough fat to see them through the juvenile period in which they learn to fend for themselves. Further, the growth of the young occurs during the time of the sudden diatom bloom and subsequent oceanic reproduction. This means that when the young are weaned and on their own, there is a maximum of food available. Even more dramatically, the harp seal (*Pagophilus groenlandicus*) requires only 10 days to almost quadruple in bulk!

Partitioning Resources

It is an ecological principle that no two species living in the same community can have the same way of life, or niche, lest competition result in the elimination of one of them. Thus, there are five species of baleen whales in the Southern Ocean, all of which eat plankton; five hair seals which eat fish, squid, and plankton; two fur seals which eat fish and krill; and several small, toothed whales and one giant toothed whale which eat mostly fish and squid; but they all have slightly different food habits and/or habitats. That is, they partition the Southern Ocean's food and space.

It is very difficult to know the exact nature of this partitioning. But over the years, some facts have emerged. The migrations of the great baleen whales to the Southern Ocean have become generally known through tagging studies. All of these whales must consume great quantities of food during intense feeding periods and they must bear their young in warmer waters. The almost blubberless newborn would probably not survive the frigidity of polar seas. To feed in polar regions and bear young in warmer seas requires migration. All whales of the Southern Ocean, therefore, migrate from warm calving grounds in temperate and subtropical waters, to rich planktonic summer pasturages. Populations of the now very rare humpback whale (*Megaptera novaeangliae*) summer near the coastlines of Australia, South America, and Africa, and certain tropical oceanic islands as well. Each population migrates to feeding grounds generally south of its summer home. There, the whales eat both fishes and a variety of plankton. Thus, the populations are separated from each other more or less year round. They also tend not to compete with other baleen whales in their feeding habits. The blue whale of the Southern Ocean is extremely specific in its food requirements; it eats only zooplankton, mostly krill. However, its Northern Hemisphere relatives are not so choosy and will eat a greater variety of plankton.

An anatomical feature of whales—the baleen—is a clue to their resource partitioning. Baleen comprises long plates hanging from the upper jaw. Baleen is formed of the same substance that produces hair and fingernails, keratin. Along its edges and at its tip, it is split finely into hair-like threads or filaments which mat together for the filtering of small zooplankton from seawater. Therefore, the baleen whales eat very small animals, which they must find in large quantities. The toothed whales, of which the sperm whale is by far the largest—but which also includes killer whales and the smaller dolphins and porpoises—feed upon the larger marine organisms such as fish.

The fact that baleen whales can successfully exploit the highly productive zooplankton of polar seas results in their being far more abundant and varied in these regions than elsewhere. The baleen whales are restricted in their feeding to the summer season when swarms of planktonic animals, crustaceans such as krill and copepods, occur. The conditions that establish these seasonally productive crustaceans have already been discussed, having to do with nutrient supply and the sudden production of subice diatoms and other phytoplankton upon which these crustaceans feed. Because the pelagic areas of polar seas have relatively little species diversity, zooplankton production is left to a relatively few species which explode into massive swarms in warm seasons, becoming a vast source of food for those animals capable of effectively harvesting their numbers. Some small fishes also take advantage of this rich food source and these fishes, in turn, can be effectively harvested by the baleen whales. The various species of baleen whales possess quite different baleen. Some possess short, coarse baleen; these whales must depend upon large plankton and small fishes, or even squid, for food. Those whales with longer and finer baleen concentrate their feeding more upon the smaller plankton. The most notable in this regard is the bowhead whale (*Balaena mysticetus*). This is the only baleen whale which never leaves ice-dominated seas. A 20-meter bowhead may have baleen of almost 4 meters in maximum length, hanging from a strongly curved, bow-like upper jaw of almost a quarter the animal's length. Another good example of partitioning of habitat and food is that of the Antarctic hair seals. The placid Weddell seal is primarily a fish-eater and mostly inhabits shorefast ice, that is, ice attached to land. The similarly colored Ross seal (*Ommatophoca rossi*) is mostly a squid-eater. It is one of the least known of all mammals and inhabits both heavy and loose pack ice, but spends most of its time in the sea and is thus difficult to observe. The most numerous seal in the world, the crabeater (*Lobodon carcinophagus*), eats krill, and lives in open, rather loose pack ice. And the leopard seal (*Hydrurga leptonyx*) is the ecological replacement of the Arctic's polar bear. It preys on fish, seals, and penguins and occurs everywhere in the Southern Ocean.

And so, the polar regions provide abundant habitat and food. But habitat alterations are rapid and food is produced briefly. Competition for resources and space is a major key to survival.

Overleaf. *A herd of caribou (Rangifer tarandus) treks across the Canadian tundra. These shaggy deer are famous for their long seasonal migrations, often traveling in herds numbering tens of thousands of individuals. During the winter, caribou head for forests south of the tundra, returning north in the spring to breed.*

The Tundra's Wide Expanses

Tundra is a Russian word for the treeless plains of the Arctic or subarctic. In other languages, the word tundra has also been applied to any treeless area in a cold climate, whether in the polar regions or on top of mountains in temperate or even tropical latitudes. The boundary that separates polar tundra and alpine tundra from areas where trees grow is called the treeline, while areas south of the true tundra are called by another Russian name, *taiga;* these areas are forested, usually with birches, spruces, and alders.

Tundra is most commonly associated with treelessness, so we may begin by defining a tree: it is a perennial woody plant, at least 2 meters tall, with a single, woody stem. (A shrub is also a woody plant, but has multiple stems.) Although the definition of a tree may appear somewhat arbitrary, there is no doubt that the treeline is very real and usually fairly distinct. The reasons for this are several: the growth and survival of trees are limited by high wind, low temperature, and shallow soils—all of which occur in polar and alpine environments.

Tundra regions can also be defined as areas where the average annual temperature is below freezing or where the temperature reaches an average of only 10°C during the warmest month, and most significant, where the ground is frozen.

Permafrost and Landforms

An aerial view of Arctic tundra reveals that it is far from a uniform landscape. Though the plant cover is low and often sparse, especially in the northernmost areas, the vegetation differs widely from place to place. This is most obvious in summer when distinctive patches of green, brown, yellow, and red appear, and when flowers bloom profusely. Without snow, the tundra reveals striking contours, due largely to the underlying permanently frozen ground called permafrost, which may extend as deep as 600 meters in the Arctic or to 1,500 meters in Antarctica. This frozen ground is impermeable to water and often contains thick layers or wedges of ground ice just under the thin layer of soil and vegetation. The vegetation insulates the soil, keeping it from thawing. If the vegetation is stripped away and a house put in its place, the frozen ground may thaw, and the house sink or tilt, much to the consternation of the home dwellers.

The freezing and cracking of the ground over permafrost causes ice-wedge polygons to form, especially in wet tundra areas. The contraction of the ground due to freezing and drying causes cracks which subsequently fill up with water, freeze, and turn into ice wedges. These wedges grow from year to year and force the ground between them upward. When the rim of the polygon is forced up, the result is a low-centered polygon with a pond in the middle. When the center is forced up, a high-centered polygon is produced.

Added to this Arctic pattern are river terraces, deeply incised river channels, sand dunes, steep banks where snow persists to form snow-bed plant assemblages, thaw-melt lakes, and pingos. The thaw-melt lakes on the coastal plain near Point Barrow, Alaska, are rectangular and are oriented northwest-southeast. Because the prevailing northeast wind is perpendicular to their axes, their lee

Named for its tufted seed head, cottongrass (Eriophorum) resembles a grass but is actually a sedge. This plant of cool to cold climates is found mostly in bogs or other wet areas.

78–79. A small group of adult male musk oxen (Ovibos moschatus) treks across the tundra of Alaska's Nunivak Island. Superbly suited for insulation against the cold of the high Arctic, the coat of the musk oxen is double-layered. On the outside are long guard hairs that drape almost to the ground; snow slides off this outer portion. Underneath the guard hairs is a layer of very fine, soft hair.

Above. *The short-tailed weasel (Mustela erminea) is found far into the high Arctic. Although by no means restricted to tundra, it eats the lemmings, voles, and similar rodents that live there. It is able to enter burrows because of its elongate shape and short legs. This weasel, which has just seized its prey, is in its white winter coat.*

shores undergo greater wave action and erosion than their windward sides. These lakes are slowly on the move before the wind.

Pingos are ice-filled hills on the treeless tundra plains; they usually bear profuse vegetation especially on their warmer, south-facing slopes. They form in shallow basins, when water accumulates and freezes, forcing whatever lies above it to higher and higher elevations. Pingos may be 50 meters or more high; how high they grow depends on their complex water balance and how well they are protected from thawing. They may assume circular, oval, or irregular forms. As they grow, plant succession progresses on them, from pioneer grasses to a shrubby mixed vegetation to a climax of whatever tundra type is locally typical. As pingos are higher than the surrounding tundra, their soils are well drained and held together by the roots of shrubs. Burrowing animals such as mink dig their homes in these dry, stable soils. These ice and soil formations are scattered across broad expanses of tundra to produce a fascinating landscape as well as an array of different habitat types for wildlife.

Plants of the Tundra

Arctic tundra is often referred to as "barren grounds" and to some it implies only a cold, treeless landscape. None of it is barren, but its species richness does decrease drastically from south to north. Of the three zones into which it is generally divided, the southernmost is relatively warm, lush, and wet low Arctic; the middle Arctic is the typical tundra inhabited by reindeer and caribou; the northernmost zone is the very cold dry polar desert where vegetation is very sparse. The low and middle Arctic tundra abounds in plants. There are about 500 different kinds of mosses and almost 450 ferns and flowering plants on the middle Arctic slopes of Alaska; the tundra near Point Barrow contains about a fifth as many species. As one goes north to the polar deserts, such as those of northernmost Canada and northern Greenland, shrubs disappear entirely, lichens become more dominant, and perhaps less than a tenth of the species diversity remains. Under more severe conditions, productivity is lowered and the plants have proportionately more photosynthetic tissues, such as leaves, and proportionately less non-photosynthetic parts, such as roots and stems.

The optimum temperature for photosynthesis in most plants of the world is 15°C or higher, whereas on the tundra, some plants have an optimum near freezing, and some, such as the tundra grass *Dupontia*, can photosynthesize at −4°C. But production of plant material is inhibited much more by the short growing season than by the low temperature. One strategy by which plants increase their growing season is a process called wintergreen, wherein leaves that might be expected to drop in the fall survive for more than a single season. For example, the evergreen leaves of pines and spruces are photosynthetically active for more than a year. Similarly, in the polar desert of northern Canada and Greenland, the majority of species of normally deciduous families of plants have been found to retain their leaves through the winter. Thus, leaves produced in one summer remain on the plant for more than a single season and are ready for photosynthetic work as soon as light and temperature increase the following spring. Were this not so, essential time and energy would be required to grow new leaves every year before photosynthesis could make its contribution, and the plants might not survive. Fortunately, there are also hardly any leaf-eating insects on the tundra to further decrease photosynthetic tissue.

Although trees are lacking, plants take many other forms on the tundra. These include deciduous shrubs such as the Arctic willow (*Salix arctica*), which is low to the ground and spreading, with leaves that turn the landscape bright yellow in the fall. There are berry-producing, evergreen shrubs such as the bearberry (*Arctostaphylos rubra*), and cushion plants such as the many saxifrages (*Saxifraga*). There are many grasses and grass-like forms, including the sedges called cottongrass (*Eriophorum*). And there are the mosses and lichens, the most cold-adapted of all, which can live the farthest north. Many of these often mingle to form a soft, yielding, soggy mat that can be treacherous to walk on. On drier ground they are more sparse.

Treeless Antarctic Expanses

If tundra is defined by simple treelessness, all polar and alpine ice-free areas of the Antarctic continent—including the dry "oasis" areas on its rim—would be tundra. But if the word also implies a coating of plants such as mosses and lichens, most of Antarctica's ice-free areas would not qualify. As for much of the life of the Antarctic region, both on land and in the sea, continental Antarctica has many plant species not found elsewhere. The Antarctic convergence also marks the southern limit of what most scientists consider Antarctic flora. The more northerly subtropical convergence is at about the latitude of the southern limits of forest. South of that boundary, from the subantarctic islands at about the latitude of the Antarctic convergence to the western Antarctic Peninsula, very few flowering plants occur, and instead, mosses predominate. In terms of plants, the rest of continental Antarctica is subdivided into a coastal area dominated by mosses, an Antarctic slope dominated by lichens, and the icy plateau where the only living things are green and red algae of the ice and snow. All in all, the exposed lands and lakes of Antarctica have only 2 flowering plants, about 75 mosses, 9 genera of liverworts, 350 to 400 kinds of lichens, 360 species of algae, and 75 species of fungi—far fewer plants than the Arctic region. Many areas remain to be explored, but it is unlikely that many additional species will be found. (An exception may turn out to be lichens that live within rock—the peculiar and not yet well understood "endolithic flora.")

In only very few locations do these plants form a ground cover even remotely like that of Arctic tundra. The Arctic polar desert is quite like Antarctica in climate, but it is still adjacent to lands to the south, whereas the Antarctic continent is isolated from all other land. It is not really certain how Antarctica's plants got there—whether they are survivors from the warmer times of long ago, whether their seeds were transported there by birds, or whether they arrived by wind or ocean current. No doubt all these processes have played a part. Even man has played his part: two species of *Poa* grass and some molds and

A short-tailed weasel surveys its territory near the McConnell River in the Northwest Territories of Canada. The weasel has a home range of about 1 hectare. It dens among piles of rocks. The female may have from four to eight young each summer. This individual is clad in its characteristic brown summer coat.

bacteria have been introduced accidentally.

Every plant has its own particular—in some cases very exacting—requirements. An old ecological principle called the "law of the minimum" tells us that, of the many factors of a particular environment, usually only the presence or absence of one or two determine whether a plant may grow in a particular spot. Thus, for one particular species, water may be limiting; for others, it is calcareous rock or soil acidity. Those plants with extremely precise requirements are called specialists, and those which can withstand a wide range of conditions are generalists. The same principles apply to animals, but since most plants stay in one place, the law of the minimum is perhaps more obvious in them.

Four principal factors determine the distribution and abundance of Antarctica's flora—climate, soil, and physical and biological factors. In all respects, the sea is of primary importance: the nearer to the sea, the warmer and wetter the terrestrial areas will be, the more salts will be brought in by sea spray, and the more nutrients will be available through the droppings and other leavings of marine birds and seals. But only on the west coast of the Antarctic Peninsula are climatic conditions at all favorable for a continuous mat of plant growth. There, the highest average summer temperatures occur—at just about freezing. Winter air temperatures generally are above −40°C, but at ground level they may be a good deal higher. Moisture is also higher there.

In most of Antarctica, little snow falls, but it is very difficult to tell just how much there is because so much of it is wind-blown. Rain is rare, but cloudy skies are frequent near the coasts. This can be an advantage to some plants, as very high radiation may be destructive to their tissues. As for the winds, those that stream off the continent are frequently of gale or even hurricane force. Snow and ice particles driven by winds also can be very destructive to plants.

The rocks of Antarctica and the soils which form from the weathering of rock are diverse. This influences plant growth; some lichens, for example, grow only on calcium-bearing rocks. The color of rocks and soils is also important; darker ones warm up faster and attain higher temperatures than lighter colored ones.

The soil of Antarctica, where it is present at all, is usually quite shallow. Some acid humus deposits occur in small pockets. On the west side of the Antarctic Peninsula and on nearby islands are banks of mossy peat almost two meters thick. They are, of course, frozen all year long. Decay and decomposition are extraordinarily slow and radioactive carbon dating has shown that their accumulation has been building for 2,000 years! Other soils are orthogenic—derived from bird droppings—and such guano-based soils are very rich in nitrogen, an essential plant nutrient. Some green algae and lichens thrive best near bird colonies.

The physical factors that influence plant growth are water availability, aspect, and snow cover. Water probably is the most important, and it must be remembered that though ice is abundant, it cannot be used by plants. The steepness of the terrain and the orientation of the slope influence both how water runs to lower areas and how much sunlight an area receives. And snow cover has

Opposite. *A large Arctic wolf (Canis lupus) stands on the wintry tundra of remote Baffin Island. On wide-open spaces of the tundra wolves may range such large territories that they number approximately one per 300 square kilometers.*

Overleaf. *Powerful, canny, and sometimes seemingly fearless, the wolverine (Gulo gulo) ranges from boreal forests to the Arctic tundra. The wolverine's fur is extremely thick. Stiff guard hairs provide protection against the polar cold, and are especially resistant to accumulations of frozen moisture.*

Above. *At their nest, two young snowy owls* (Nyctea scandiaca) *hold brown lemmings* (Lemmus trimucronatus) *in their bills. These owlets are white and will soon fledge. Snowy owls usually live where trees are absent, and nest on the ground in a slight depression scratched out by the female. Lemmings are its main food; when lemmings thrive, so do the owls. When the lemming populations drop, however, the owls suffer. Lack of food may send large numbers of these birds south to the temperate regions of the United States and Central Eurasia.*

Left. *A young snowy owl still wears some of the brown plumage in which it began life.*

Lupine flowers (Lupinus arcticus) *bloom on the tundra. The lupines are an especially hardy group of plants that belongs to the pea family. They can tolerate the acidic soil of the treeless Arctic barrens. The scientific name* Lupinus *means wolf-like, a reference to an old but erroneous belief that the plant robbed the soil of its fertility.*

several advantages to plants. If the land slopes toward the sun, snow is more likely to melt and supply water to local plants. Snow also insulates plants from wind, low temperature, and from the sun's harmful ultraviolet radiation. Some algae and lichens photosynthesize better under the reduced light of about a third of a meter of snow than they do in full sunlight because too much radiation inhibits photosynthesis.

The biological factors are exceedingly diverse. Basically, if a plant exists in an area at all, we must assume that it has evolved to meet local climatic conditions and has acquired specific adaptations. We have already spoken of wintergreen and increased photosynthetic tissue. Another remarkable adaptation of plants lies in their ability to alter growth form. For example, the lichens are the most widespread plants of polar regions. There are three major growth forms: *crustose* lichens are encrusting, usually on rocks; *foliose* ones are leaflike in form; and *fruticose* ones are branching. Lichens are the only plants which can colonize bare rock surfaces, and some survive in Antarctica at −75°C. They can grow well below freezing temperatures and best from 0°C to 20°C. They are resistant to drying and some species can also grow while saturated or even submerged. In the relatively lush areas on the west side of the Antarctic Peninsula, one lichen, *Usnea*, covers rocks and ground in blackish, moss-like tufts. Only there, and on nearby islands, where mats of mosses and Antarctica's only two flowering plants also occur—the grass, *Deschampsia antarctica*, and an herb, *Colobanthus crassirostris*, which is closely related to the chickweeds (*Stellaria*) of North America and Eurasia— can a tundra vaguely reminiscent of the Arctic region be said to exist.

Invertebrate Life on Antarctica
We have spent much time on plants because they are essential for all other life. They are the producers, whereas the animals and nonphotosynthetic bacteria and fungi are the consumers or the decomposers. Only in the high tundra of the polar desert or on the most exposed peaks are invertebrates totally absent. Over most of the Arctic, many insects, in particular, occur. But in Antarctica, very few insects exist and the situation is far simpler than in the Arctic. Its mountainous topography and the narrowness of its ice-free coastal area means that animal life is as sparse and patchy as that of plants. However, many small terrestrial organisms are present in large numbers in a few locations. The invertebrates that are able to exist in Antarctica depend upon the availability of water more than all else, which means they must have microhabitats that stay above freezing at least part of the year. Such temperatures are also necessary for the production of the plant matter on which the vast majority of them live. Most of them inhabit the soil, and the minimum soil moisture required for their existence is apparently about 2 percent.

The microscopic soil animals include protozoans, round worms, and others called rotifers and tardigrades, but the predominant species are insects, mites, and protozoa. There are a couple of dozen species of mites, one of which is Antarctica's only land predator, *Coccorhagidia*. There are less than ten springtails and a flightless fly called

Belgica antarctica. The latter, with a body about 4 millimeters in length, is the largest terrestrial animal there. *Belgica* breeds in brackish coastal lakes and ponds. The mites and springtails generally inhabit shallow soils, mosses, areas under rocks, and crevices between boulders and gravel. The mites are extremely resistant to freezing and drying, and neither the mites nor the springtails exhibit seasonal reproductive periods; they just breed whenever conditions permit and become dormant whenever conditions are harsh.

Near the coasts, where vegetation is most abundant, there are habitats favorable to a variety of animals, from protozoans to insects. Within this habitat of tufts and mats of mosses the springtail (*Cryptopygus antarcticus*) is the largest (2 millimeters) and most abundant organism. It may reach average population densities of over 60,000 per square meter in some places, but the total weight of even this many is less than a gram. *Cryptopygus antarcticus* eats a variety of algae, fungi, detritus, and soil microbes at a rate of about 2 percent of its body weight a day. This springtail probably accounts for at least half of all the metabolism of larger soil animals, demonstrating how very important such small organisms can be in these very simple ecosystems. Even so, its contribution does not approach that of the protozoans and bacteria.

The dry valleys of Antarctica are too dry to support insects, but there are places in the mountains far from the sea where some melting of ice provides water. In gravelly, rocky places which seem lifeless, rare rock-lichens grow in cracks; some of these are enolithic forms, mentioned above, which are currently under study by scientists. These mountainous places, which are the most remote habitats for terrestrial life on Earth—as far south as 86° South latitude and as high as 3,600 meters in altitude—appear to be remnants from preglacial times. Some of the peaks where springtails, such as *Antarcticinella monoculata,* are found may never have been covered by ice.

The mite, *Nanorchestes antarcticus,* occurs in the same southerly habitat. Its powers of cold resistance are spectacular—it can withstand up to −41°C without freezing!

Resistance to Cold

Tiny insects and mites are at the mercy of their immediate environment. They cannot migrate, nor can they be very active most of the year; thus they are common only where temperatures rise above freezing. Conditions suitable for their activity occur only on about 60 to 100 days a year; the rest of the year they are dormant. Since growth at low temperatures is relatively slow, those species with smaller body size have a better chance of maturing in a single season; hence, mites, such as *Nanorchestes,* are about a quarter the length of the millimeter-long mites of the northernmost rim of Antarctica.

Cold resistance is just as well developed in the Arctic as in the Antarctic, but a great many more invertebrates inhabit Arctic tundra. Bumblebees and flies pollinate Arctic flowers and there are several kinds of bloodsucking insects as well. Beetles and spiders are prominent consumers and predators. Some of these can tolerate

Carrying a mouse that it has killed, an Arctic fox (Alopex lagopus) peers through the low foliage of the Pribilof Islands in the Bering Sea. The fox has two color phases, blue and white (although only the blue phase occurs on the Pribilof Islands). During summer, when this picture was taken, both varieties are brownish to gray. The fox has adapted to Arctic life in several ways. In winter it may obtain food by following polar bears, scavenging their kills. It also eats dead marine animals washed up on the ice or shore. When rodents emerge from hibernation in spring and summer, the fox turns hunter as well as scavenger.

extremely low temperatures. In the summer some far-northern insects may resist freezing only down to −6°C, a fairly high level for polar regions. But in the fall the lower limit is gradually extended down to about −60°C. This astonishing capacity is the result of the insect's production of glycerol-like antifreeze substances that penetrate its cells. Apparently a slow rate of cooling is required—less than 1°C a minute—to allow the insect to achieve its maximum resistance.

Animal Cycles on Arctic Tundra

The supposedly "suicidal march" to the sea of the European brown lemming (*Lemmus lemmus*) is legendary. And although a movement of animals does occur, the popular explanation is partly fanciful. Research confirms that their mass migrations are probably the result of overpopulation. When these animals encounter water, they will attempt to swim across, risking drowning or predation.

This baby gyrfalcon (Falco rusticolus) *will grow into one of the most efficient hunters of the Arctic. A true bird of the north polar regions, gyrfalcons shun forests in favor of the open tundra and seacoast along the northern fringes of North America and Eurasia.*

In order to understand this behavior of lemmings and their population cycles, one must study the whole ecosystem because lemmings are sensitive to overcrowding, food shortage, and other alterations. Lemmings are animals of the tundra which make extensive burrows with several chambers about 10 to 15 centimeters in diameter, and line their nesting chambers with fur. It is probable that the burrowing activity of these lemmings aerates and loosens the tundra soil, encouraging growth of such plants as grasses and sedges. Since the fresh shoots of grasses and sedges are the major food of lemmings, they may be said to "till their own garden," which enables them to collect and store more food for the winter months. Lemmings also eat the bark and twigs of willows and birches when there is a scarcity of their preferred food.

When lemming numbers are high—up to 200 per hectare—they are the predominant herbivores, consuming a large percentage of the available forage. But every 3 to 5 years lemming numbers collapse to about one animal per hectare and their impact on the ecosystem becomes insignificant. Lemmings graze by clipping grasses and sedges near the ground surface, and as shoots are produced below this line, new leaves continue to grow. But when the lemming density becomes too great, the shoot-producing parts of the plants are eaten and even the roots are dug out. This destroys the plants and the protective cover of the soil, which is thus subject to erosion as the sun heats and melts the frozen ground.

No one knows exactly why these cycles occur, but a current hypothesis is as follows. Early in a peak lemming year food is abundant and lemming nutrition is high, but as their numbers increase over the summer, food quantity decreases and nutrients such as calcium and phosphorus become tied up in organic matter, such as the lemmings themselves and their droppings, so that food quality also decreases. The soil thaws deeply where plants have been overgrazed by lemmings and by the end of summer masses of lemmings die. The following year the lemming population is at a low ebb and forage material is of poor quality since decomposition has not yet completely released organic nutrients back into the soil. By the third to fifth year the forage quality has improved, and the soil

Top. *An adult gyrfalcon on Seward Peninsula, Alaska, displays the sharp, hooked beak with which it tears the flesh of its prey. The diet of this bird changes with the seasons. In winter, it feeds on Arctic hares, snow buntings, and ptarmigans. Gyrfalcons that live near the sea may also prey on oceanic ducks. During the summer, the bird has a much greater choice of prey, including lemmings, ground squirrels, and even geese.*

Bottom. *An adult gyrfalcon tends its young in Brooks Range, Alaska. The gyrfalcon requires an elevated location for nesting, preferably a rocky ledge that is shielded overhead by an outcrop.*

has again become insulated by both dead plants and new plants. Then, the population peaks once again, and the stage is set for another population collapse.

Thus the old explanation of lemming migrations and numbers as the result of the psychological effects of overcrowding appears to be only a part of the picture. We now suspect that the lemming cycle can be understood only in terms of their whole ecosystem, in which soils, nutrients, vegetation, and the lemmings themselves all play a role. Nor does the story stop there. Since many other herbivores compete with lemmings for food, they too are affected. So are predators such as the snowy owl, the short-eared owl, the rough-legged hawk, and the pomarine jaeger, whose numbers and movements fluctuate in response to the lemming cycle. Both sandpipers and Lapland longspurs utilize the bones and tooth fragments of lemmings as sources of calcium; they may benefit when the lemmings die off. Hence, some animal populations may flourish as the lemmings decline in numbers.

Tundra Birds and Mammals

A multitude of birds and mammals inhabits northern tundra. As we have pointed out, most of these, such as songbirds, owls, hawks, ptarmigans, and shore birds, are invaders from more southerly climates. Some songbirds are truly Arctic, notably the circumpolar snow bunting (*Plextrophenax nivalis*), which forages in small grassy patches as soon as the snow melts. But most characteristic are the raven (*Corvus corax*) and the snowy owl (*Nyctea scandiaca*).

The raven is a playful opportunist. In northern villages it takes the place of the city pigeon, scavenging whatever it can find, even in garbage dumps. Its size, heavy-whiskered beak, and wedge-shaped tail distinguish it from crows, to which it is closely related. Ravens do aerial acrobatics, including barrel rolls and loop-the-loops, and they jostle other ravens while in full flight. They make a number of croaking and melodious sounds and appear to talk to themselves in flight or while perched.

The snowy owl is stately rather than playful. It flies in moth-like silence, hunting for its prey of small rodents, mostly lemmings, and it breeds on the open tundra, laying 5 to 7 white eggs in a dry, grassy depression. When the lemmings die off, snowy owls travel far south in their search for food, and one can tell when lemmings are scarce in the north by the sudden appearance of snowy owls in temperate zones.

The mammals range in size from shrews weighing only 4 grams to the moose which weighs over 600 kilograms. They include rodents such as muskrats, lemmings, ground squirrels (used by Eskimos for clothing and hence sometimes called "parka squirrels"), as well as foxes, wolves, hares, lynxes, wolverines, weasels, otters, caribou, moose, and musk oxen. The lemmings are the commonest rodents on the wet Arctic plains, but related voles (*Microtus*) share their habitat and are even more common in some places. The total population of small rodents may reach as many as 500 per hectare. For the larger rodents, such as the Arctic ground squirrel (*Spermophilus parryii*), densities may be 7 per hectare. But for caribou or reindeer (*Rangifer*), local censuses may

approach one for every 4 hectares, and average perhaps no more than 7 per square kilometer. But even this may be high, and their abundance may change drastically with the seasons or with migration.

Surprisingly, there is only one true hibernator on the tundra and that is the Arctic ground squirrel. Most small tundra mammals store their food for the winter. They lack the ability to become torpid in the cold, and so remain active all winter long. These little animals all live under the insulative snow in winter. Each has its own habitat requirements—marshes, wet meadows, polygon troughs, well-drained ridges, uplands, or even the few areas that remain snow-free.

Large mammals, of course, cannot live beneath tundra. Bears make winter dens, but the rest are active in the open throughout the winter. It is highly characteristic of all such animals to be very wide ranging. Tundra is not very productive and it is rich only because it is so vast in area. It is important for large herbivores, such as caribou and musk oxen, to range widely because they would rapidly overgraze their habitat if they did not. They may also be forced to travel when snow is moved about by the wind. Whenever snow consolidates into a hard surface, the plants below may not be available for grazing; caribou and musk ox must dig through winter snow for their food and so are very sensitive to the hardness of frozen ground. This is less true of moose (*Alces alces*) because they browse in aquatic areas or on twigs which project through the snow. The moose is less an inhabitant of the tundra than the caribou, the former being more at home in the spruce and muskeg. Caribou regularly venture to the taiga, especially when tundra winters produce hard snow and little available food.

Wolves and Their Prey

The wolf (*Canis lupus*) is a highly intelligent and social animal. It travels in packs, hunts cooperatively, and is gentle to others of the pack. It has a complex language and even has its own equivalent of a "smile." The tail between the legs indicates submission. Ears laid back and teeth bared is a threat. Tail held high in a curl over the back indicates confidence. Indeed, the wolf's language, by howl or by body posture, is far more complex than that of any domestic dog. Wolves are skilled predators and their relationship to their prey is still under investigation. They are not wasteful predators, killing more than they can eat, and only when caribou or moose numbers are low do wolves have a serious impact on their populations. The wolf is highly territorial, one pack frequently covering more than 250 square kilometers in its hunting forays. When traveling, wolves maintain contact by means of "assembly howls," to make known their location or to signal arrival at a point of rendezvous. A "lonesome howl" indicates a wolf separated from the pack. Packs generally avoid each other and herbivores are subject to least predation on the pack's territorial boundaries. The wolf is socially one of the most interesting of animals; its gentle family behavior is surely worthy of imitation.

The caribou (*Rangifer tarandus*) is closely related to the domestic reindeer (*Rangifer rangifer*); in fact, the two probably comprise a single species. They are both highly gregarious, sometimes traveling in herds of many

Above. *Red and green mosses grow thickly on Bathurst Island. Low plants such as Bryum are better able than tall plants to survive the impact of wind and cold on the wide-open tundra. Mosses require moisture, which is abundant on the tundra in warm weather. During the arid winter, they form clumps, enabling them to conserve what moisture is available. Red Bryum typically grows on the very edge of streams.*

thousands. Caribou are speedy runners—up to 80 kilometers an hour—but they cannot maintain such speeds for long, especially in summer when they would become overheated. Their large feet help in travel over snow. They are good swimmers. They take to water or lie in the snow to avoid bloodsucking insects. They are mainly lichen-eaters, and reindeer moss is named for them.

The moose is a huge, mostly solitary, ungainly looking animal. Males weigh over 600 kilograms and antlers may spread almost 2 meters from tip to tip. They are not as speedy as are caribou, but are unpredictable in behavior and formidable due to their size and strength.

The musk ox (*Ovibos moschatus*) is the strangest of the large herbivores. It is a shaggy beast which possesses a very fine wool—even finer and longer than cashmere. This wool is actually underfur and is shed in great patches in summer, when it may be collected and woven into fine scarves and sweaters. Musk oxen form herds—smaller than those of the caribou—of from 3 to 100 animals. The basic social unit consists of the cow, her newborn calf, and her yearling. When approached by wolves, musk oxen form a circle; they face outward and hold their heads low. Their young stay in the middle of the circle. The adults will attempt to toss the wolf into the air with their horns —which are found on both sexes—and crush the attacker with their feet. Against all of these, the wolf is still formidable, but it is little wonder that it often resorts to hares and mice.

Above. *Arctic bearberry* (Arctostaphylos rubra)—*a member of the heath family— grows on the Alaskan tundra. Most bearberries are low-growing plants. Several species, including the one shown here, are common in Arctic and subarctic regions.*

Opposite. *By late August, autumn hues have splashed the vegetation of the Alaskan tundra. Arctic bearberries ripen, and the leaves of the ground-hugging Arctic willow* (Salix arctica) *turn yellow. By the beginning of September, the first cold storms come, and shortly thereafter, winter will grip the land.*

Wildlife of Mountain, Glacier, River, and Lake

Over much of the polar regions, little of the snow that falls melts. (On the average, 30 to 60 centimeters fall annually.) In the vast snow and ice fields and in mountain valleys, the resulting net gain produces—or has produced—ice sheets or glaciers, moving masses of ice. Simply stated, the conversion of snow to ice is a matter of recrystallization under pressure. When snow accumulates to 20 or 30 meters in thickness, its weight exerts enough pressure on the lower layers to melt and recrystallize them into glacial ice. At an even greater depth and with more pressure, the ice is forced to flow. When snow accumulates in a mountan valley, any ice subsequently formed flows river-like, down the valley. The lowest and outermost tip of the glacier may be subjected to above-freezing temperatures and melt; this produces a river of icy water. Or the glacier may flow into the sea where chunks of ice calve from its terminus to float out onto the seas as icebergs. In the case of ice sheets—as in Greenland or the Antarctic—the flow is very generally outward from the center toward the periphery of the land mass.

Life on Peaks, Cliffs, and in Dry Valleys

By no means do snow and ice cover the entire polar landscape even in winter. Snow cannot accumulate on steep slopes or cliffs and no snow at all accumulates in parts of Antarctica called oases.

The climate of mountains and cliffs is not only a matter of large-scale effects of wind patterns and air temperature. The rugged topography has the effect of creating many microclimates which differ widely according to variations in slope and aspect. Wind is highly variable over short distances. If a high mountain slope faces south in the Arctic, it will receive much more sun for a longer period than the adjacent flat tundra. If plants cover the ground, that ground will be better insulated than if it is bare. And, bare rock surfaces respond much more rapidly to solar heating than crevices between rocks, which maintain a relatively constant temperature and humidity. The result of all these variables is that lichens that coat rocks, cushion plants that contribute to tundra-like alpine flora, and invertebrates such as mites have very patchy distribution among the slopes and cliffs of mountainous areas.

The willow ptarmigan (*Lagopus lagopus*) and rock ptarmigan (*L. mutus*) are the northernmost grouse. Both nest on the ground and turn from a mottled brown and white in summer to pure white—except for the black bills, claws, and tail—in winter. The black eye-bar of the rock ptarmigan distinguishes it from the willow ptarmigan; the former is more of an upland bird than is the willow ptarmigan, which prefers lowland tundra. These birds require much energy for survival—up to a fifth of their weight in food every day in the form of berries and vegetation.

Preying on such birds as ptarmigans, are falcons, among the most spectacular of fliers. Both the peregrine (*Falco peregrinus*) and the largest of falcons, the gyrfalcon (*Falco rusticolus*), nest on rugged cliffs. Their long, pointed wings and long tails give them great speed. They do not soar for long periods like the chunky rough-legged hawk (*Buteo lagopus*), but fly with a series of short, rapid

98. *Spreading out like a fan, a glacier moves down a valley; its movement is controlled by slope, shape, and pressure. As the slope increases and the valley narrows, the ice moves more rapidly. Some glaciers in North America advance, others retreat. Glaciers advancing at speeds of more than 30 meters a day have been recorded near the coast of Greenland.*

100–101. *Above Alaska's North Slope, mountains in the Brooks Range tower over Lake Udirvik. The Brooks Range stands at a latitude at which all land is north of the treeline, even at sea level.*

Above. *Mountains of the Brooks Range rise in the midst of Alaska's vast William O. Douglas Arctic Wildlife Range, the home of grizzly bears, wolves, wolverines, caribou, Dall sheep, and myriad birds. Summering on the Arctic tundra north of the Brooks Range are hundreds of thousands of geese, swans, old squaw ducks, eider ducks, and many other waterfowl.*

Opposite. *Dall sheep* (Ovis dalli) *feed on slopes and in ravines at dawn and early morning. They climb higher to rest during midday, and resume feeding again in mid-afternoon. When winter cloaks the mountains in snow, the sheep forage on ridges, which are swept clear of snow by the wind.*

wing beats on their hunting forays and cover much ground in doing so.

The falcons are mostly bird-eaters and literally knock their prey from the air in spectacular dives called stoops. The magnificent gyrfalcon is a permanent Arctic resident. It has two color phases; one darkly mottled and the other snowy white, spotted with gray and black. It is somewhat more flexible in its food habits and hunting methods than the generally migratory peregrine and will take rodents on the ground as rough-legged hawks do.

The Dall sheep (*Ovis dalli*) symbolizes American Arctic mountains best. This relative of the bighorn ranges south into Canada and in its white color phase is abundant in Alaska. The rams bear spectacular curved horns which are quite different from the bony antlers of moose, caribou, and deer. These horns, like claws, hooves, fingernails, and baleen, are composed of keratin. Whereas antlers are usually shed annually, the horns of both male and female Dall sheep grow continuously, but in seasonal spurts; hence, the horns bear seasonal rings called *annuli*, which tell the age of their bearer. It takes about 7 years for the male's horns to grow to a full circle, spiraling around the side of its head. Among males, the function of the horns is to establish social dominance. Their horn-ramming battles are well known.

Dall sheep are very agile and wary. They keep a sharp watch for wolves, wolverines, bears, and men. They prefer rugged, relatively dry areas where alpine meadows are interspersed with precipitous terrain. They feed in the meadows on alpine and tundra plants and can dig through snow for food. But if the snow and ice become too heavy for the sheep to dig through, some of them may starve. In May and June, pregnant females seek the solitude of the most inaccessible places to bear their lambs. The lambs feed on vegetation as well as milk soon after birth. By late summer they are quite independent of their mothers. By late fall, the period of sexual excitement, the females are in heat and the rams in rut. Usually, females in heat mate only with the dominant ram of the area.

There is not much wildlife in the mountains of Antarctica. Mountain peaks called *nunataks* emerge like rocky islands from a sea of snow and ice, some bearing a beautiful growth of brightly colored lichens. But no birds nest there and no sheep wander about. In fact, the more remote places appear to be utterly devoid of life and appear to be as sterile as the surface of the moon. Only near the periphery of the continent are the mountains much inhabited by plants and a few insects, protozoans, and mites; exceptions are the springtail and mite described in chapter two. One might expect the dry valleys at the western side of the Ross Sea to be glacier filled since they nestle between snow-covered mountains. But there is little snow and ice in them and they may be the driest places on our planet. The moisture is so low that only a few lichens and some soil bacteria can grow there. Life is generally inhibited by high desiccation rates, low temperature, high soil salinity, little organic matter in soil, short growth periods, high levels of ultraviolet radiation, and frequent freeze-thaw cycles. Yet even in the face of these extreme conditions, some life prevails. In one dry valley an intensive study revealed that, even in this remote and inhospitable area, molds and spore-

Top. *A Dall ewe rests with her 2-day-old lamb. Lambs are born —usually in late spring—after a gestation of 180 days. Birth occurs on isolated, inaccessible ledges or crags. The lamb is able to walk, although not well, in a few hours. Before it is a week old, the young sheep can negotiate the rugged, steep rocks on which its elders live.*

Bottom. *The Dall ram remains with his fellow males during the summer; adult males form a herd apart from females and young. By fall, however, the male seeks out mates, trying to gather as many females for himself as possible. A ram competes for the right to a female by battering its huge horns against those of its opponent until one ram tires.*

forming bacteria have been introduced as a result of human activities.

On a plateau near the dry valleys, where jumbled assemblages of rocks, known as *felsenmeer,* occur snow may be trapped. This snow melts because of the rock's heat absorption under solar radiation, even at air temperatures below freezing. Fine, wind-blown particles are also trapped there. Thus, both soil and water are present and enable mosses to grow.

One other sign of life in the dry valleys and their environs is the mummified remains of seals. These are shriveled corpses, mostly of young crabeater seals. Radioactive carbon dating shows these carcasses to be of varying ages, up to several thousand years old. Surely the seals never really intended to be there but were blocked from the sea by ice. Unable to reach open water, they wandered into this dry valley region where no vertebrate can survive for long.

The Snow Flea

Among the organisms with a remarkable capacity to survive in snow-covered areas are springtails, insects of the order Collembola. These are primitive creatures with little rounded heads, segmented bodies, and a spring on their tail which aids them in making giant leaps forward. Snow fleas—they are really not fleas at all—are found in temperate climates in soils, forest litter, and areas under rocks and logs where they feed on detritus and other small particles. For many years, some species have been known to leave the litter of the forest floor in winter to emerge onto the snow surface a half meter or two above. But until three decades ago, only one was known to inhabit snow fields at the tops of glaciers. This one was known from Switzerland; its name, *Isotoma nivalis.*

As it turned out, its relatives frequent snow and ice fields widely throughout the Northern Hemisphere, including the polar regions. None occurs, however, in Antarctica.

In spring, when the melting season on the snow fields begins, and the snow begins to show pink, orange, and red tinges of the algae *Chamydomonas nivalis,* multitudes of snow fleas appear. Some relatives of *Isotoma nivalis* itself are right out there in the middle of the snow field; the rocks are far below under hundreds of meters of snow and ice. The habitat of this tiny, millimeter-long insect is a vast jumble of new-fallen snow and thawed and refrozen *firn,* sometimes known to skiers as "corn snow" because of its rounded shape and dense texture. Each of these particles is like a boulder to the little snow fleas. Through a magnifying glass, they can be seen crawling over and among the particles and, if poked with the tip of a pencil, they will leap a distance 20 times the length of their bodies, by means of the spring on their tails.

Snow fleas subsist on particles such as pollen which are blown onto the snow fields from nearby tundra or forest areas in spring and summer. No pollen or other detritus is produced on snow fields of Antarctica; this is probably why no snow fleas occur there.

The snow fields where *Isotoma nivalis* lives are the birthplaces of valley glaciers. These snow fields and glaciers, which get warm enough at their surfaces to melt a little in spring and summer, may send water down a

Tundra merges with the Brooks Range. The range is crowned by Mt. McKinley, which, at 6,190 meters, is the highest peak in North America. Because of altitude, tundra on McKinley is very similar to true Arctic tundra found farther north.

short distance into the snow and the porous or crevassed ice below, producing a surface flow of water over the more solid ice. In other cases, the glacial ice may be porous enough to permit water to permeate to such an extent that a veritable river emerges from beneath the leading edge of the glacier. In either case, water percolates down through the snow field to warm the snow to isothermal—the 0°C freezing point of water and melting point of snow and ice.

Even during winter many snow and ice fields thaw a little by day and freeze again at night, when unseasonal warmth occurs. This thaw-freeze process increases in spring, is at its greatest in summer, and decreases in frequency in the fall. It is a process that produces ice bands in the snow. Also, in autumn snow begins to fall and may, in some places, accumulate to several meters depth by winter's end.

Now, picture the snow flea. Millions of them, perhaps as many as 1,000 per square meter, may inhabit particularly favorable snow fields in summertime. Their blackness aids them in warming because of absorption of solar radiation. But with the coming of fall, their activity decreases and they are buried by snowfall. They must possess some of the same antifreeze defenses as other insects, but they may also remain active. In any case, they must avoid being blocked from the surface by ice bands in the snow. Furthermore, how do snow fleas detect springtime under their thick snow blanket? A possibility is that the life of *Isotoma nivalis* is keyed to the isothermal conditions of thawing. Trickles of water through the snow may be sufficient to arouse it. If so, the snow flea could scramble upward from time to time and avoid becoming buried too deeply. When spring comes, the snowfleas might even be just beneath the surface, ready for pollen to appear.

Lakes and Ponds

Arctic lakes echo with cries of loons and waterfowl in summer, but those of Antarctica are silent and most of them are permanently covered with an icy mantle. The Arctic loon (*Gavia arctica*) nests on tundra lakes and utters a variety of cawing, wailing, and honking cries. Its nearest relative, the red-throated loon (*Gavia stellata*) is more silent, quacking only from time to time. It also is a tundra lake nester but usually chooses smaller and shallower lakes than does the Arctic loon. Both are large birds, 60 centimeters in total length. But a fourth again larger and much heavier is the common loon (*Gavia immer*). All loons are highly territorial; only one pair inhabits a single pond.

It is the waterfowl—ducks, geese, and swans—that are most numerous on the tundra's ponds. There is a large array of northern tundra birds, most nesting on the tundra itself, but the waterfowl are most strongly associated with the ponds which they use for nesting and for escape from terrestrial predators such as the Arctic and red foxes, which take large numbers of adults and young annually. The life histories of these waterfowl are well documented, but their migrations are especially worthy of mention. Many species of waterfowl make migrations of thousands of kilometers from Arctic tundra where they breed, to temperate lakes, bays, estuaries, lagoons, and coastal areas where they winter.

Above. *Jagged chunks of ice swirl in the Hulahula River, located between the Beaufort Sea and the Brooks Range. After being carried by the current for some time, the pieces of ice gradually melt. Into rivers such as this, Arctic char come from the sea to breed in summer.*

Opposite. *Boulders are sometimes picked up by glaciers and carried for many kilometers before being deposited. As they travel, they become rounded and smooth. Such boulders are called "glacial erratics."*

Above. *Rivers and streams like this one on Ellesmere Island sometimes spring from the melting ice of a glacier. Many of the streams that flow from glaciers start deep within the ice in tunnels formed by erosion as the glacier moves over the ground. Meltwater from atop and within the glacier seeps into these tunnels, making the watercourses increasingly larger.*

Opposite. *Most widely distributed of all loons, the red-throated loon (Gavia stellata) nests in ponds and small lakes on the Arctic tundra. The nests are constructed of mud and vegetation.*

The swans and geese are long-lived and most mate for life. Some individuals are often found in the same tundra ponds and wintering areas year after year. In the north, ideal conditions exist for breeding, due to the immense numbers of ponds and small lakes. Many waterfowl are as territorial as loons, each pair occupying a pond of its own. After hatching, the precocial young, as well as adults, feed on the abundant insect life of the ponds and new, protein-rich shoots of both aquatic and tundra plants. By late summer, the young are as large as their parents and are able to fly. The decreasing day length and the freezing of ponds require that flocks go south where they will find other abundant food sources. These migrations require great energy. But they also must occur when conditions are timely and correct at both ends of the long migration. To migrate thousands of kilometers northward, only to find the tundra ponds still frozen, is like traveling to the waterhole in a desert oasis to find the well dried up. The same is true at the other end of the migration; after a long flight south, the birds must find suitable feeding and resting areas, not dredged, filled, or polluted by human enterprise. Their existence, therefore, is tied to two widely separated habitats. The number of waterfowl in the world is greatly diminished because not enough attention and international cooperation has been given to this migratory aspect of their lives. Exceptions to depletion do occur as exemplified by the explosion in numbers of Canada geese that inhabit Chesapeake Bay in winter.

No birds nest in the lakes of Antarctica. Low temperatures and climatic aridity are the major factors which limit the number of lakes and their suitability for life. There are several distinct kinds of lakes. There are a few permanently frozen ones in the mountains; a few lakes even occur 3,000 to 4,000 meters under ice. No life is known to occur in either of these types of lakes. Around the rim of the continent, lakes occur in the dry valleys mentioned earlier in this chapter. The composition of lakes of these areas varies widely, from fresh water to water containing salts of over a dozen times greater concentration than seawater. Some of the latter have freezing points depressed to less than −40°C. In some places this is below the mean winter air temperature, so the lakes never freeze. Summer heating by solar radiation may raise the temperatures of some of these lakes to 17°C; one of them even reaches 25°C, possibly being heated by geothermal sources as well as by the sun.

Other lakes of Antarctica occur on coasts and nearby islands; some of them are of marine origin. Finally, there are lakes of the Antarctic Peninsula and offshore islands, some of which derive nutrients from colonies of penguins and seals. The principal life of these lakes consists of algae, 70 percent of which are the primitive "blue-greens"; these are closely related to bacteria, both being classified as procaryotes, i.e., the nuclei within their cells are not bound by an enclosing membrane. Bacteria, blue-green algae and other forms of algae combine, forming algal mats, also called felts, because of their texture. In some lakes, aquatic mosses make a significant contribution to the flora, but in none is the phytoplankton bloom very significant. Many small, mostly microscopic invertebrates —protozoans, rotifers, and worms—occur whenever algal

Top. *Although the blue phase of the snow goose* (Anser caerulescens) *was once considered a separate species, frequent occurrence of mixed pairs such as this one is evidence that the color phases are, in fact, a single species. Snow geese breed in ponds and lakes on the Arctic tundra from Northeastern Siberia to Greenland.*

Center. *Brant geese* (Branta bernicia) *leave the coastal waters of western Europe and North America in late spring, traveling far north into the Arctic above 74° latitude. There they breed on lonely beaches, marshes, and especially islands. The nest is constructed in a slight depression and lined with mosses, lichen, and the birds' own down. These birds seldom stray far from the ocean, even in breeding season.*

Bottom. *A pair of snow geese wades through the shallows, followed by their goslings. These birds seem to stay with the same mate for life. They breed on tundra near coasts in the high Arctic. They forage in marshes and shallow ponds for waterweeds and at the water's edge for grasses and sedges.*

mats occur. In a few of the warmer, richer, more northern lakes, crustaceans are also abundant. For example, the small freshwater ponds of Signey Island, in the South Orkneys near the top of the Antarctic Peninsula, are relatively temperate compared with most Antarctic lakes. They have 1 to 2 meters of ice for eight to eleven months a year. Nevertheless, almost a dozen species of crustaceans occupy some of them. Most of these graze on algae. One huge copepod, *Parabroteas sarsi*, is 7.5 millimeters long, and can capture, kill, and eat the grazers, some of which are nearly half its size. In such lakes, a relatively complex food web may be said to occur. No one has yet managed to determine the entire pattern of nutrient cycling of these ponds, but they are almost ideal sites for such studies, as most are almost totally closed ecosystems; that is, little enters or leaves the lake's confines (with the exception of those lakes near penguin or seal rookeries where feces are major nutrients).

Underwater Life of Arctic Lakes

Arctic lakes are richest in species the farther south they occur. Phytoplankton species are numerous and productive in some lakes and, as in the case of marine diatoms described in chapter two, they are able to photosynthesize at very low light levels under the ice from late winter onward. Also, as for the sea, the productivity of phytoplankton is much greater than zooplankton, so that there is also an inverted pyramid of biomass. Most of the crustaceans which feed on phytoplankton breed but once a year or even less because of the short growing season. Some take more than a year to mature and the various species may spend the winter in egg, immature, or adult form.

The fishes of these northern lakes feed on the zooplankton, but because of the general low productivity of the higher latitude lakes, especially, it is dubious that they could survive on zooplankton alone. The Arctic char (*Salvelinus alpinus*) of the high Arctic eats mostly insects. Since insects and their larvae occur seasonally in the Arctic, landlocked char eat seasonally, and may live 40 years or more, growing very slowly.

A most remarkable Arctic fish is the blackfish (*Dallia pectoralis*). This is a mudminnow, and other members of its family, Umbridae, occur in the temperate parts of the United States and Europe. But the blackfish is exclusively Beringian, occurring in Eastern Siberia, the Bering Sea islands, and the low-lying tundra ponds and streams of Alaska. Mudminnows are so named because of their preferred habitat of low-lying, mossy, or sphagnum-filled ponds with soft bottoms. They like to burrow there for protection, and a good way to collect them is simply to gather large globs of pond debris, dump it on the bank, and look for the tell-tale wriggles of fish.

The blackfish is somberly colored, dark green to brown with darker speckling. It may reach almost 30 centimeters in length and is the commonest of fishes where it occurs. It spawns in spring and summer when temperatures reach 10 to 15°C. It feeds on almost whatever it can find in the way of crustaceans, insects, mollusks, and worms. Astonishingly hardy, it can withstand complete absence of oxygen for a day, if kept at low temperature, and can go without food for a year. Its tolerance for cold is legendary.

Above. *Much of the time the moose* (Alces alces) *feeds in the relatively deep water of ponds, lakes, and marshes. It wades far out from shore, dipping its head, or even diving under the surface to obtain water plants.*

Left. *A moose sends a shower of droplets into the air as it shakes off water after coming up with a mouthful of food. Although the moose likes to feed in aquatic areas, it also browses on willows and other woody plants in forested areas and on mountainsides.*

There is an old tale that a frozen blackfish was eaten by a dog, then thawed in the dog's stomach, to be vomited up alive. This tale is dubious, but the blackfish's tolerance to cold is a fact. It is not certain how this tolerance is achieved. Blackfish will survive −20°C for about three-quarters of an hour if only parts of the body are frozen—presumably nonvital parts. Complete freezing kills them. It appears that antifreeze in the blood, avoidance of ice crystals, burial in debris, and the production of great quantities of mucus about their bodies prevent them from freezing in winter.

Life in Arctic Rivers

Many large rivers enter the Arctic Ocean and subarctic waters from North America and Eurasia. All have highly seasonal flows, usually silty waters derived from snow, ice, and glacial melt. Their fish species are dominated by the trouts and their relatives, the salmon, whitefishes, and grayling. Pikes, smelts, cods, and others either inhabit these rivers all year or ascend them from the sea to spawn. A number of these have become land-locked or have become inhabitants of large lakes. The grayling (*Thymallus arcticus*) and northern pike (*Esox lucius*) are notable lake-dwellers and also occur in temperate waters. A great many of these northern fishes are much-sought sportfishes.

The sheefish (*Stenodus leucichthys*), or inconnu (French for "unknown"), is entirely Arctic and subarctic in North America and Siberia. The inconnu may weigh 25 kilograms, and is a strong fighter on a line. In spite of the female's production of 100,000 to 400,000 eggs, its strict spawning requirements keep its populations limited; it must have 1.3 to 2.6 meter-deep water with a fast current over a bottom of variously sized gravel. It spawns in early fall and grows rapidly compared to other Arctic fishes.

The Arctic char (*Salvelinus alpinus*) is the most northerly trout. It looks superficially like the salmons, being also pink-fleshed, but is related to the brook and lake trouts. It migrates from the sea to spawn, as do the salmon, and the juveniles remain in fresh water for 3 to 4 years before returning to the sea. Unlike the Pacific salmons, which have similar habits, the Arctic char does not die after spawning. It often becomes landlocked.

Thus we see that for a variety of reasons the life of the habitats considered in this chapter is far richer in terms of species variety in the Arctic than in the Antarctic. The lakes and glaciers of the northern polar regions comprise complex ecosystems while those in the Southern Hemisphere support only a few organisms whose ecological relationships are as yet little known. The same is true of mountainous and glacial terrains.

114 top. *The harlequin duck* (Histrionicus histrionicus) *lives year-round throughout much of the Arctic. It inhabits mountain streams and also spends considerable time on the ocean.*

Bottom. *A red phalarope* (Phalaropus fulicarius) *dives for food in the shallows off Southampton Island, in Canada's Northwest Territories.*

Opposite. *An Arctic char* (Salvelinus alpinus) *lies just under the surface of a shimmering stream on Baffin Island. The char is the northernmost freshwater fish.*

Overleaf. *The delta of a glacier on Bylot Island, Canada, is laced with braided streams, runoff from the ice.*

On the Edge and Floor of Polar Seas

The edge of the sea forms the union of two very different habitats, the land and the sea. Such a union between two habitats is called an *ecotone,* and the seashore ecotone is inhabited by a great variety of living things, for it possesses some characteristics of the sea, some of the land, and some that are uniquely its own. Many of the inhabitants, both plant and animal, have colonized it from the sea or from the land, while many others, adapted to its unique conditions, are found nowhere else. The extent of this coastal ecotone and its species is not confined to the shoreline itself. Water near the shore is fed by countless freshwater streams, while seabirds that nest on the shore may forage on the ocean hundreds of meters away; the influence of the land thus extends far out to sea. In the opposite direction, the coastal zone extends as far as salt spray is carried by the wind, to produce maritime conditions far inland.

The polar coastal zones, both land and sea sides, are as varied as coastal zones are anywhere else on Earth. There are sandy shores and high cliffs interspersed with barrier beaches, estuaries, and lagoons. There are beds of sea grass and kelp, and a variety of rocky, sandy, and muddy sea floors. The coastal zone, perhaps because it is an ecotone, is also the most productive zone on our planet. It is utilized by many fishes, such as herring, Arctic cod, salmon, and char. Even more striking is its bird life: the largest known concentrations of birds are to be found there.

Ice-Stressed Coasts

In most polar regions, both sea and glacial ice scrape and scour the shores, crushing or uprooting shallow-water, attached species, such as sea grasses, kelp, and barnacles. Ice of glaciers carves out fjords and erodes shorelines. Sea ice forms pressure ridges that gouge out troughs and mix the upper layers of sediment. Near the shore, the sea bottom is often coated by crystals called anchor ice, which form on the sea floor as they do on the undersurface of ice. In the Antarctic, in particular, many benthic animals may be trapped in this anchor ice when masses of it are detached from the bottom and float to the undersurface of the sea ice above.

Under such stresses, it is astonishing that anything at all survives. But much does, for the destructive action of the ice is not the same everywhere and the ice at least has the beneficial effect of lessening the impact of waves that lash ice-free shores. The tidal fluctuations of polar seas are also generally slight and are further moderated by sea ice. All this has the effect not of eliminating bottom-dwelling, or benthic, life in shallow water, but of causing a zonation of organisms. Within this zonation, life adapts to a variety of environmental conditions which are produced by stresses of various sorts on the slope of the shore as it descends underwater.

In heavily ice-stressed areas, no barnacles can grow because they cannot move. But the intertidal Antarctic limpet, *Patinigera,* moves to upper levels during ice-free summers to feed on algae, and then moves down beneath the ice in winter. This limpet avoids scouring of ice and also protects itself from freezing by coating itself with mucus containing an antifreeze that effectively prevents ice from penetrating its tissues. The periwinkle snails

Above. *An Adélie penguin incubates its egg in the midst of a blizzard. The male penguin incubates the eggs for about 2 weeks while his mate feeds at sea. He does not feed until she comes to relieve him. In another 2 weeks the male returns for a final round of incubation.*

(*Littorina*) found both in north temperate and Arctic regions can also move to avoid ice, but can survive at −15°C; these snails have adapted to such cold by becoming dehydrated, preventing the formation of lethal ice crystals within their cells.

As for plants, an abundance of diatoms and filamentous green algae live on ice-stressed coasts between high and low tide levels, but these survive there only in ice-free summers. They must withstand desiccation, low temperatures, and intense solar radiation. Beds of eelgrass (*Zostera marina*) are able to grow in quiet Arctic lagoons where ice scouring does not occur. Here eelgrass can survive the dark winter under a layer of ice. One bed, in Izembek Lagoon in the southern Bering Sea, is the largest eelgrass bed in the world. Most surprising, perhaps, is an encrusting Antarctic lichen, *Verrucaria serpuloides*, which occurs at depths as great as 10 meters. It is the only lichen that is entirely marine.

Marine algae are colored green, red, and brown, and are filamentous, blade-like, or lettuce-like in shape. They range in length from less than a centimeter to over 100 meters. Polar species seldom exceed a half-meter in length. They are attached to pebbles and rocks by structures called holdfasts, but they have no roots. Although they are very sensitive to ice scour, several species occur in the ice-stressed coastal zone. Whole communities of fishes and invertebrates may depend on them, directly or indirectly, just as, on land, birds and mammals depend on forests. Most Antarctic algal forests occur in the vicinity of the Antarctic Peninsula, but good algal stands also occur in the western Ross Sea, as far south as heavily ice-stressed McMurdo Sound.

Aside from ice stress, three factors appear to dominate the distribution of Antarctic algae: latitude, suitable substrate, and water depth. Generally, there are fewer species farther south. Of the approximately 350 species of marine algae known from the Southern Ocean—many of them found nowhere else—over half are restricted to potentially ice-stressed areas 10 meters deep or less. About 20 percent of these occur in deeper water; 10 percent occur only from 10 to 37 meters, and 23 species occur only below 37 meters, where light levels are very low. Some of the latter such as *Ballia callitricha*, a filamentous form 15 centimeters in length, cannot live where the intensity of light is high. The known limit of algal growth is 668 meters, a remarkable depth for a photosynthetic plant, even in clear Southern Ocean waters.

In the Arctic, there are far fewer of these large algae and most are invaders from temperate seas. There are many reasons for this, including sea ice, a lack of hard substrates on which to attach, and generally murkier water, due to the input of silt-laden rivers, than that of the Southern Ocean. One large brown alga, *Laminaria solidungula*, a kind of kelp, occurs in the Canadian high Arctic. This kelp grows fastest in spring under the thick ice. Its growth is dependent on the availability of nitrogen, and is not correlated with light levels.

The Sea Floor

The floor of the sea, or benthos, has many attributes in common with terrestrial environments. Its sediments are

123 top. *An Adélie penguin constructs its nest of pebbles on Signey Island, part of the South Orkney Island group. Adélies sometimes steal nest-building stones from one another.*

Center. *A nesting gentoo penguin confronts an intrusive sheathbill (Chinois). Although sheathbills are primarily scavengers, they may raid penguin colonies, breaking eggs, eating their contents, and snatching up chicks. Sometimes several sheathbills will mob an adult penguin that is feeding its youngster, pecking it until it gives up the food.*

Bottom. *On Elephant Island near the Antarctic Peninsula, a chinstrap penguin (Pygoscelis antarctica) feeds its youngster. Penguins catch fish and invertebrates, swallow them, and then disgorge them for their offspring to eat.*

Overleaf. *A troop of Adélie penguins toboggans across the Antarctic ice toward the sea. By pushing themselves along on their bellies, Adélies sometimes travel faster than on foot.*

123

Top. *Adélie penguins rocket up onto an ice floe. They swim so fast as they approach a floe that usually they pop out of the water and land on their feet.*

Bottom. *Hurling themselves out of the water, Adélies "porpoise" through Hope Bay, Antarctica. This practice enables them to breathe without interrupting their progress. Penguins sometimes reach speeds of 25 kilometers an hour in the water.*

Above. *Adélies leap into the sea from the ice. They often enter the water in large groups, possibly to minimize the danger to individuals from the leopard seal* (Hydrurga leptonyx) *and other predators.*

Overleaf. *The stripe under its chin identifies this chinstrap penguin* (Pygoscelis antarctica) *as it spreads its wings on the shores of Paradise Bay, Antarctic Peninsula.*

much like soils in many respects, providing substrate in which animals may burrow and where plants, such as the sea grasses, may take root. Like soil, these sediments contain nutrients, and the organic matter is consumed by benthic animals in much the same way that earthworms consume soil organic matter. Many benthic animals—such as most oysters, clams, barnacles, and sea squirts—use the substrate only for anchorage, feeding entirely on plankton that they filter from seawater. Others—like most shrimps—feed on particles or detritus that drift to them, or accumulate on the bottom.

The Arctic benthos is mostly comprised of a wide continental shelf. Where wave action is slight and the bottom is largely muddy, worms, mollusks, and small crustaceans are common. Where there is considerable wave action, and the bottom is rocky or gravelly, algae and sponges are dominant. In some of these areas, the number and variety of species may be quite low, but there may be a high biomass, nourished by under-ice diatoms as we noted in chapter two. The higher into the Arctic one goes, the less these species depend on diatoms because of the shorter growing season, and the more they must depend upon detritus and small organisms carried to them by rivers or currents. Farther south, filter-feeders predominate. In fact, normally filter-feeding species of mollusks may become detritus-feeders in high Arctic waters.

The Southern Ocean has a greater variety of benthic animals than do Arctic and subarctic waters. The well-nourished waters of the eastern part of McMurdo Sound have also produced greater densities of benthic animals than almost anywhere else on Earth. Great density and variety does not mean that productivity is also higher; in McMurdo Sound, productivity undoubtedly is not high, since these waters have only a brief period of phytoplankton production each year. But the "standing crop" of benthic life is exceedingly diverse and numerous, being almost twice as rich in numbers of animals as some temperate estuaries and over a dozen times richer in biomass than some locations off Bermuda.

Most Antarctic invertebrates have low reproductive rates. They produce a small number of large yolky eggs that hatch into bottom-dwelling larvae, without the intervening planktonic stage usually found in warmer waters. Some have exceedingly slow growth rates. Some sponges grow to very large sizes—as large as the huge basket sponges of the tropics which are large enough for a person to sit in. In 10 years of observation, growth of some sponges could not be detected. One can only guess at their ages, but they could be centuries old.

Sponges are an abundant and dominant form of life in McMurdo Sound, in terms of sheer biomass. One of them, *Mycale*, is potentially the dominant animal of the community, as it will grow over and smother other attached invertebrates. It is fast-growing, and not restricted by lack of space; however, it is relatively rare. The reason for this appears to be predation by two starfishes, *Perknester* and *Acodontaster*, and by the shell-less snail *Anstrodoris*. The sponge's defense is mucus secretion, but this is not entirely effective in deterring these predators. What then prevents the elimination of *Mycale*? The answer is predation by yet another, smaller

Top. *An octocoral*
(Dendronepythya) *grows in the
chill waters of New Harbor,
McMurdo Sound, Antarctica.
Octocorals include sea pens, soft
corals, and sea whips. Most of
them live in warm waters, but a
few thrive in cold seas.*

Bottom. *A sponge* (Class
Demospongea) *stands almost a
meter high in McMurdo Sound.
Sponges flourish in polar waters,
constituting the bulk of the
biomass in some places.*

Opposite. *A "garden" of animals
that resemble plants grows
profusely under a rock cleft in the
Antarctic Ocean. Growing here
are several soft corals and sea
anemones as well as sea
cucumbers and echinoderms, a
class that includes sea stars and
sea urchins.*

starfish, *Odontaster,* which kills the young of the
predatory starfishes as well as the shell-less snails and
their larvae in its detritus-hunting wanderings. This web
of predation evidently keeps the system in balance.
Should pollution occur, *Odontaster* might gain the upper
hand, reducing the numbers of *Perknester* and
Acodontaster; Mycale would then become dominant in
biomass.

Coastal Marine Mammals
The sea otter (*Enhydra lutris*) and the several species of
fur seals are really inhabitants of high temperate—or low
polar—seas. Nevertheless, they do live within the
boundaries of the polar seas, as we have defined them in
chapter one, although they have not adapted to them as
completely as have the hair seals and the walrus which we
will discuss in the next chapter. Sea otters and fur seals
exploit many of the same food resources as the polar hair
seals, whales, and penguins. And they have some
remarkable adaptations of their own to cold.
The sea otter is the largest member of the weasel family,
larger even than the wolverine. It is most common along
the coast of the North Pacific, to the Aleutian Islands at
the southern boundary of the Bering Sea. The northern
fur seal (*Callorhinus ursinus*) migrates to the Pribilof and
Commander Islands at the edge of the Bering Sea's
continental shelf where over a million seals feed on pollock
and other fishes. Most southern fur seals are not polar,
but one of them, the Kerguelan fur seal (*Arctocephalus
gazella*), gathers on subantarctic islands to bear young
and feeds on krill, far south of the Antarctic
convergence.
These fur-bearing species were all drastically reduced
during the nineteenth and early twentieth centuries; most
notably, the sea otter was thought to be extinct but was
rediscovered in the late 1920's. All are now protected by
international agreement. All are coastal, though fur seals
spend much of the year at sea. The sea otter inhabits
rocky coasts where kelp beds are often extensive. It
seldom comes ashore, but it can move about easily on
land. The fur seals must come ashore to breed, and they
have good powers of land locomotion. The large males
establish territories on beaches near the sea and
vigorously defend them, and any females in them, from
other males. All these animals have true fur, as opposed
to hair, and have little blubber, unlike other marine
mammals. "Fur" means that there is a dense coat of
underfur overlain by longer guard hairs. There are
more hairs on a square centimeter of a sea otter's body
than there are on an entire human head. The fur seal's
hair density is only slightly less. So dense is this fur that
the skin beneath it is unwettable. When these animals
enter the water, the guard hairs and underfur are laid
back and trap air; consequently the animals' bodies are
insulated against the cold. Because such air-filled
insulation is compressable and will lose its effectiveness at
great depths, sea otters and fur seals seldom dive much
below 30 meters, although they can go deeper for brief
periods. Such fur must not be soiled, lest the fur becomes
matted and the animals lose their insulation. They
constantly groom themselves, and oil pollution poses a
severe threat to them.

136–137 top row left. *Small arthropods, such as this member of the family Acanthonotosomidae, thrive in the cold waters of the Southern Ocean.*

Center. *Sea spiders inhabit cold oceans from shorelines to the depths. This animal (probably Nymphon australe) has an enormous proboscis, tipped by a mouth, which it inserts into the soft bodies of coelenterates such as hydroids and sea anemones to suck out their vital juices. These animals have no notable abdomens; their digestive organs are located in their legs.*

Right. *The largest Antarctic isopod is* Glyptonotus antarcticus. *Isopods are crustaceans, most of which are aquatic.*

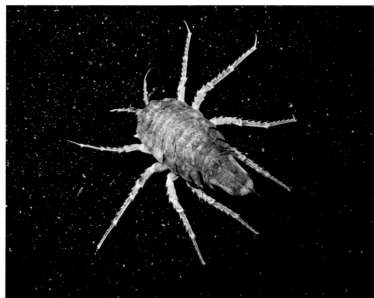

Bottom row left. *Nudibranchs, such as* Duvaucelia challengeriana, *are brightly colored mollusks without shells. They feed on coelenterates. The stinging cells of coelenterates are devoured and may be stored in the naked gills of the predator's body. The cells retain their stinging qualities and provide defense for the nudibranch.*

Center. *The five arms of serpent stars* (Ophiurolepis) *are brittle but very flexible. These animals range from tropical to polar waters, and from near shore to the depths. There are some 1,600 different species, many having bodies only 25 millimeters in diameter.*

Right. *This octopus belongs to one of two Antarctic genera,* Graneledone *or* Pareledone.

Bottom. *Isopods, such as* Microarcturus, *have the jointed, hard exoskeletons characteristic of arthropods.*

Overleaf. *A member of the Antarctic cod family,* Trematomus challengerians, *prowls near a green sponge* (Latrunculia apicalis) *in McMurdo Sound. Sponges of this species are found only in the Antarctic and subantarctic islands. The bumps covering the surface of the sponge contain pores that let in sea water, which is filtered for tiny marine plants and animals. The bottom-dwelling* Trematomus challengerians *feed on small crustaceans.*

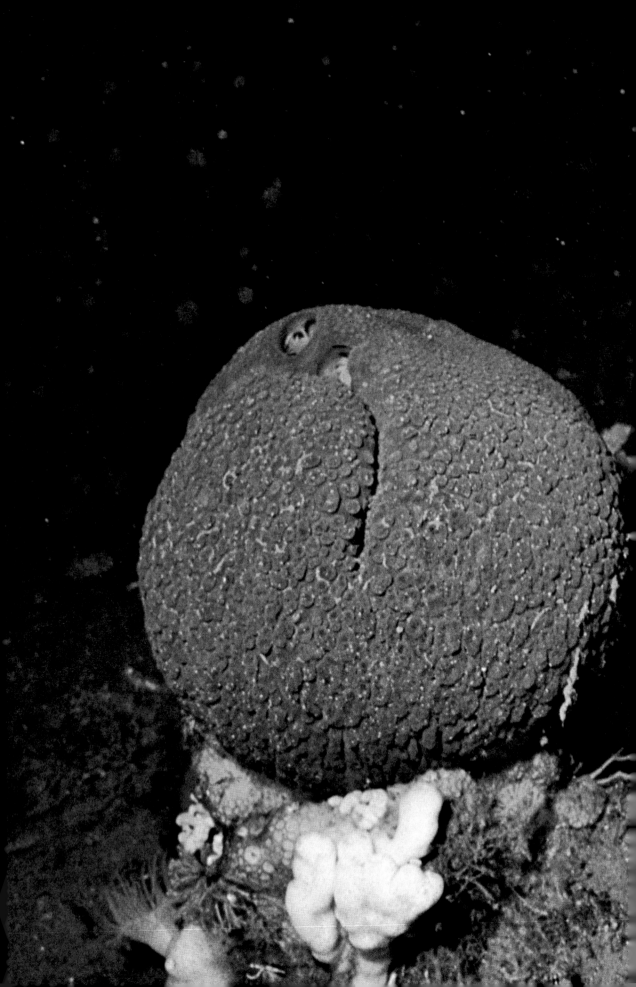

The sea otter is a benthic feeder and its appetite is so great that it may consume food that equals 25 percent of its body weight a day. Its compensation for cold is partly a high metabolic heat production—hence its appetite. Sea otters eat clams, sea urchins, and other invertebrates. Sea urchins eat kelp and kelp forests provide a habitat for many other species. The presence of sea otters reduces the number of sea urchins and this helps promote dense growths of kelp; the sea otter's absence may result in many sea urchins, little kelp, and smaller numbers of kelp-inhabiting animals. A species that so markedly influences its own habitat is referred to as a keystone—a name derived from the top stone in an arch that prevents it from collapsing.

Finally, several temperate zone species of hair seals invade polar regions. Most notably, the southern elephant seal (*Mirounga mirounga*) breeds on the same South Atlantic subantarctic islands as do fur seals and penguins. This largest of the seals is ungainly on land. Knowledge of its life at sea is very scant. It is probably a deep diver that feeds on a variety of squid and fish. Males weigh as much as 1,800 kilograms, are over 6 meters in length, and have a long, overhanging nose. The females are only a little more than half the male's length and weigh less than 460 kilograms. Like fur seals, they breed on shore; single males may mate with a dozen or more females. Several other hair seals also inhabit northern shores and inshore boreal waters, most notably the harbor seal (*Phoca vitulina*) and the gray seal (*Halichoerus grypus*). They lead lives similar to their ice-inhabiting relatives described in the next chapter, but usually use beaches, rather than sea ice, for breeding and resting. Thus, their excursions in the sea are much more limited.

Birds of Land and Sea

Of all the animals of polar regions, none are more conspicuous than birds of the sea and shore. There are oceanic birds such as albatrosses and their relatives the petrels, prions, and shearwaters. There are coastal and oceanic cormorants, gulls, skuas, kittiwakes, terns, auks, murres, puffins, and guillemots. There are the strictly shore-adapted birds—the sandpipers and their relatives, including the odd Antarctic sheathbill (*Chionis alba*). And there are the seven species of truly Antarctic and subantarctic penguins. Only two, the Adélie and emperor, are exclusively continental. The other five—the king, chinstrap, gentoo, macaroni, and rockhopper penguins—are maritime or peripheral to the Antarctic continent. Sea and coastal birds have evolved many behavioral, physiological, and anatomical mechanisms to cope with the extremes of polar environments and to enable them to exploit the sea while rearing young on land. Their distributions are controlled largely by the availability of adequate nesting sites and distribution of their food. Most coastal birds and seabirds nest on islands or cliffs. Puffins, petrels, and prions need soil to make burrows; the murres, guillemots, and kittiwakes are mostly cliff-nesters, occupying narrow ledges on which they lay their eggs; the auklets often nest among rocks on steep slopes. Nesting sites may be in short supply for some; ice-clad Antarctica offers only a few bare places where the Adélie penguin (*Pygoscelis adeliae*) may establish its colonies.

Opposite. *Black-legged kittiwakes* (Rissa tridactyla) *and razorbill auks* (Alca torda) *gather on a rocky North Atlantic coast. Vast numbers of seabirds, often of several different species, together colonize rocky coasts and islands. Some of the colonies contain millions of individuals.*

141 top. *Parakeet auklets* (Cyclorrhynchus psittacula) *of the northern Pacific, Bering Sea, and western Arctic Ocean feed far out in the ocean and usually come to land only to nest.*

Bottom. *The crested auklet* (Aethia cristatella) *roves the northern Pacific and Bering Sea. It rears its young on sea cliffs and in mountainous areas not far from the coast.*

Perhaps this limitation is what has forced the emperor penguin (*Aptenodytes forsteri*) to form its breeding colonies on thick, shorefast sea ice. Some birds are limited by other factors. The wind and waves are important to larger albatrosses for soaring on their long, narrow wings. Near sea ice, waves are suppressed, so the albatrosses do not venture far into polar regions in the presence of ice. Many of these birds fly over the water searching for food near the surface. A few, notably some of the shearwaters (*Puffinus*), pursue their prey for short distances underwater; they are good fliers and also use their wings to propel themselves underwater. However, flying and true diving are not really compatible. Flying birds have too great a buoyancy to swim well, while deep divers, like the auks, murres, and puffins, are heavier-bodied birds, with reduced powers of flight. One, the extinct great auk (*Pinguinus impennis*) was totally flightless, as are all penguin species. The penguins are very heavy-bodied and have sacrificed flying for the ability to exploit deep-water food.

Although there are few studies on the effect birds have on the marine ecosystem, it must be significant. In the western Ross Sea along the 1,100 kilometer coastline from Ross Island to Cape Adare, there are 24 Adélie penguin colonies, numbering about 600,000 birds. It is estimated that these birds make foraging trips of approximately 300 kilometers each way to find food. Thus, the colonies exploit areas of about 330,000 square kilometers. Only about a half a square kilometer is available per bird. This seems like a lot, but one must keep in mind the keen competition with seals and whales for food in the same area.

How Birds Adapt

Migration is more characteristic of birds than of any other group of animals. The great colonies of northern auks and kittiwakes migrate south in winter, some only as far as the ice front where oceanic resources are relatively abundant. Others travel great distances, most notably the Arctic tern (*Sterna paradisaea*), which nests in the high Arctic and winters in austral and south polar regions. There, Arctic terns inhabit sea ice, where they avoid competition with other terns such as the resident Antarctic tern (*Sterna vittata*). The Wilson's storm-petrel (*Oceanites oceanicus*) is another long-distance migrant, crossing the Equator to spend its nonbreeding season in the oceans of the Northern Hemisphere.

The penguins are the most restricted in migration as they must walk or swim. Adélies may march in little groups over ice for days to reach their rookeries in the spring. Their ability to navigate is remarkable. In winter they inhabit sea ice close to its front. Sea ice drifts eastward around the continent, and yet the birds are able to compensate for this, returning not only to their colony, but to the very nests where they bred the year before. They travel on foot and navigate by taking readings on the sun; they become somewhat disoriented when the sky is overcast.

Feathers are a fine insulation. But they are not nearly as effective as fur. Further, birds are of relatively small size compared to mammals and do not have as thick a layer of blubber. Therefore, polar birds, like the common

Above. *A tufted puffin* (Lunda cirrhata) *stands on a rock on St. Paul Island in the Pribilofs. Puffins dig burrows about 1 meter deep in the soil-covered slopes near shore. They may also breed in rock crevices. The male and female take turns incubating the eggs and feeding fish to the young.*

Opposite. *Horned puffins* (Fratercula arctica) *range the North Atlantic coasts. The puffin's large beak helps it catch and hold several fish at a time. Puffins and similar seabirds seem to "fly" underwater, rather like penguins, but unlike penguins, they can also fly in the air.*

murre (*Uvia aalge*) and the thick-billed murre (*U. lomvia*), compensate for relatively poor insulation by means of high metabolic rate. Chicks do not achieve a stable internal body temperature until they are nine or ten days old and require constant brooding by their parents.

At times, even in polar regions, birds do get too hot. They must then dissipate body heat or their internal temperature may rise to the lethal point. The giant petrel (*Macronectes giganteus*) is as large as some albatrosses. Its normal internal body temperature is 39°C. There are blood vessels that run to the feet where there are dense networks of interconnecting capillaries. By increasing blood flow to the feet, heat is dissipated and the bird is able to cool itself. At the other extreme, when the temperature outside falls to 0°C, the exposed and unprotected feet can be the location of a loss of heat. However, the bird has a mechanism that conserves heat. The arteries of the leg lie close to the veins; thence, the warm blood going to the feet is cooled by the returning cool blood that has circulated there. Heat is further conserved by a reduced blood flow to the leg resulting from thickening of the blood due to the cold and restriction of the small capillaries of the foot.

Continental Penguins and Their Predators

The emperor penguin is in many ways among the world's most peculiar cold-adapted birds. It is found only on continental Antarctic shorefast ice, and does not nest as far north—to the maritime peninsular region of the Antarctic—as does the other solely continental nester, the Adélie penguin. The emperor seems to break many commonsense rules. It has deserted land for shorefast ice to incubate its eggs; it lays its single egg in the dead of polar winter; and it fasts for three months during the coldest weather in order to hatch that single egg by springtime.

The feathers of the emperor, as in other penguins, are tiny, and almost scale-like. There are no spaces between patches of feathers—such as occur in other birds—except in the area of the brood patch, located between their feet. These feathers form a kind of "shell" that keeps water from touching the surface of the skin. Under these external feathers, for further insulation, are finer, almost hair-like feathers called filoplumes. In late May, after the emperors have accumulated fat reserves, they congregate on thick shorefast ice near continental shores. Soon after they arrive, in the darkness of polar night, the female lays a single egg which the larger male immediately tucks away on the top of his feet and under a flap of skin that covers the egg like a blanket. The female then leaves to spend two months feeding at sea. There is no territorial behavior. Rather, the incubating males pack themselves tightly together, so much so that only about 20 percent of their body surfaces may be exposed—except for those less fortunate birds on the periphery of the group. The bird can shuffle about a bit, carrying the egg, which hatches in 60 to 65 days. During incubation, the male may lose 40 percent of his weight. Soon after the egg hatches, the female returns from the sea to care for the chick. With her return, the male leaves to feed in the sea. During the spring, the chick is fed by both parents, and by December

150 top. *A fulmar* (Furmarus glacialis) *flies near Semidi Island, Alaska. Fulmars feed on small marine animals and carrion.*

Bottom. *Like their Antarctic relatives, great skuas* (Catharacta skua) *of the Arctic are quarrelsome birds. These birds are fighting over food that they have pirated from another bird.*

Opposite. *An Arctic tern* (Sterna paradisaea) *incubates its eggs. This bird breeds on coasts throughout the Arctic and subarctic.*

Overleaf. *Arctic terns leave north polar regions in the fall and migrate approximately 15,000 kilometers to the seas fringing the Antarctic.*

it is fledged, just at the time when its sea ice home begins to break up. Therefore, the emperor penguins spend half a year with their egg and chick. Why so long? The larger the bird, the longer hatching and growth take. The little Adélie accomplishes incubation and fledging in half the time of the emperor. One can only be curious about an extinct penguin of the Pleistocene, a 125-kilogram relative of the emperor; how long did it take this giant bird to raise its young?

The nesting habits of the Adélies are somewhat more conventional. The birds begin nesting early in the spring, each pair placing their two eggs on a simple platform of stones. As in the emperor penguin, the male Adélie takes the first incubation shift, while the female feeds at sea. After about two weeks, the female returns to relieve the male, and in another two weeks the male is back for a final round of incubation. The young are brooded by the adults for about three weeks, and depart from the colony to fend for themselves about a month and a half after hatching. During this long period of incubation and fledging, south polar skuas (*Catharacta maccormicki*), giant fulmars, and sheathbills are ever on the alert to snatch up unattended eggs and chicks; losses to these predators occasionally run as high as 80 percent of the young, but this situation is rare. Penguin species can endure heavy losses of young because once the birds are safely at sea, mortality is very low, and adults can live for more than 20 years. In fact, skuas may even benefit Adélie survival. The skua is a highly territorial bird that keeps others of its kind away from portions of a penguin colony within its territory. The result is that only a few skuas prey upon any one colony of penguins. These few have very little impact.

The leopard seal is the best-known penguin predator. Individuals are ever on the prowl near penguin colonies. The penguins group on the shore, carefully inspecting their prospects for an unhindered dash to the sea. Then, as a group, they plunge in and rapidly swim. The birds are much more agile than the seals, but among the broken bits of shore and sea ice, the seal is difficult to detect. Penguins are snapped up and quickly killed, then shaken into bite-sized pieces. Though seals take many penguins, their depredations on the colonies are apparently not severe.

Oceans of Ice

The ice-inhabiting seals and penguins, the notothenioid fish, and all the unique creatures of polar seas live in an environment little known to man. It is estimated that the most numerous deep water invertebrates of the polar seas are squid, yet some species are known only from beaks found in the stomachs of seals and whales!

To understand the sea, and the life in it, we need to look downward, vertically, through layers that make up the complex and constantly moving levels of the sea. Each layer merges into the adjacent one without entirely losing its continuity. This layering is determined largely by density differences, or weight per unit volume of water, which is largely determined by the salt content of water and its temperature. The more salt in water, the heavier it is; the higher the temperature, the lighter it is. Thus, fresher and warmer water is usually found at the surface; saltier and colder water is usually at the bottom. Within each "water mass," as these layers are called, are communities of organisms which are adapted to its salinity, temperature, and to permanent darkness below a few 100 meters depth. Although there are no walls or floor as we know them on land, the pelagic, or oceanic, sea is thus clearly subdivided by characteristics of water.

Cornerstone of Polar Oceans

During the cold and dark of polar winter, there is little primary phytoplankton production under sea ice or in the polar waters. Therefore, the animals—that is, the zooplankton—which depend upon phytoplankton are not themselves active or productive. The zooplankton are the major food resources for the life of these seas. They are mostly crustaceans such as the copepod *Calanus* of the north and the shrimp-like *Euphausia* of the south. Each of these spends the winter in deeper water. They rise to the surface to feed when the ice-associated or midwater phytoplankton bloom occurs. Some copepods have high metabolism only during the periods of phytoplankton abundance which may cover only a month or two. They may drift in one direction in deep water in winter and in the other direction in surface water during and after spring and summer feeding. By rising to the surface in spring to feed and by sinking to relative dormancy in fall, they maintain their distribution in a narrow latitudinal band. Remarkably, the various species of Antarctic crustaceans, such as krill, exist in separate latitudinal bands in the Southern Ocean. This, in turn, determines the distributions of animals which prey upon them. A consequence of their short feeding season is that some zooplankton species can breed only every second year. Adults usually produce large, yolky eggs which hatch into large young in time for the spring bloom. And both adults and young store high-caloric fat to carry them through the winter.

No ecosystem on Earth is so well-delineated, perhaps, as that of the Southern Ocean. Its northern limit is the Antarctic convergence and its most notable living feature, the animal which best characterizes it is the crustacean known as krill (*Euphausia superba*). This is the major food source for many Southern Ocean species. Scientists are just beginning to comprehend how the Southern Ocean ecosystem works, and the dynamics of krill is surely a major aspect of it. This species is found in

greatest abundance where the concentration of nutrients and other processes favorable to the production of its phytoplanktonic food occur—mostly in the Southern Ocean south of the Atlantic. It feeds by filtering phytoplankton from the water by means of a "filter basket" formed when the animal extends its legs forward, downward, and outward. In summer, great swarms of krill inhabit waters less than 10 meters from the surface, both in open water and among loose pack ice. Some single swarms have been reported recently to comprise 10 million tons in biomass—the equivalent of about 2 million elephants! The distributions of animals that feed on krill—including fishes, penguins, seals, and whales—obviously depend upon the availability of these massive supplies. Some scientists have estimated that there are at least a third of a billion metric tons of krill as a "standing stock" in the whole Southern Ocean. Of this, crabeater seals (*Lobodon carcinophagus*) consume an estimated 100 million tons. In the days before commercial whaling, however, whales were more numerous and consumed much more than now, perhaps even more than is now taken by the crabeaters. As the whales were depleted, the crabeater seals, the krill-eating penguins, the Kerguelan fur seal (*Arctocephalus gazella*), and perhaps some fish species probably grew in numbers. However, they require quite different amounts, and also different species, of krill. Whales require only an estimated 4 times their own body weight of krill per year; crabeaters may require 20 to 25 times their body weight, and penguins up to 70 times their body weight. This is a consequence of the ratio of body surface to body mass; the higher this ratio is, the more food is lost as heat rather than stored as body material. So a 100-ton blue whale, the largest creature on Earth, requires 400 tons of krill per year, but 100 tons of penguins require 7,000 tons of krill! The result of man's whaling has probably been that a much smaller biomass of seals and penguins is eating the food that the whales formerly consumed. For every whale, there is now probably only about a fifth as much weight of seals and a twenty-fifth as much of penguins within the Southern Ocean ecosystem—a much less effective use of the Southern Ocean's production processes.

This does not mean that the Southern Ocean ecosystem itself is in jeopardy. What it may well mean is that an "altered stable state" may now exist in which the giant whales may never regain former abundance. They now must face keen competition from the faster reproducing populations of their replacements. But as the Southern Ocean and its inhabitants depend so extensively on krill, another thought is, what if the krill were to be decimated? Would this result in yet another stable state, or would such a key species be struck that stability itself would be threatened? Scientists are still far from the answer.

A Sea Ice Home

Sea ice is used as a stable substrate by animals with former ties to a land existence. Marine mammals have evolved from land mammals; they have readapted to the sea and have evolved a body form similar in appearance to that of fishes, while retaining certain characteristic mammal-like features. Fur seals and sea lions, for instance, still bear young on land while the walrus may

154. *In the chill Antarctic waters, a Weddell seal* (Leptonychotes weddelli) *emerges from under the sea ice. To facilitate breathing and emergence onto the ice, this pinniped has an effective method of enlarging natural openings in the ice. Moving its head from side to side, it saws the ice with its upper canines and incisors.*

156–157. *Harbor seals* (Phoca vitulina) *frequently inhabit fjords in subarctic waters. There they take advantage of ice carved from glaciers. The waters of the fjords provide food, and the ice facilitates escape from land-based predators.*

158 top. *A female hooded seal* (Cystophora cristata) *watches over her pup. The female nurses her pup for about 3 weeks; at that point, the pup is weaned and the mother leaves it to fend for itself. During this 3-week period the male remains near the female in order to breed when nursing is over. These Arctic seals are solitary animals; they are rovers of deep water far from shore.*

Center. *A Weddell seal rests with her youngster on the Antarctic ice. In spring, the wind chill factor may approach −40°C. During high winds and blinding snow, the pup remains on the lee side of the mother and keeps warm against her belly.*

Bottom. *At birth, harp seals* (Pagophilus groenlandicus) *are wet and stained yellowish with fluids, which rapidly freeze. As the pup moves about, the frozen fluids fall off, revealing a coat that is fluffy and white. Approximately 2 weeks later the white coat begins to shed and is replaced by a gray, spotted one. Young seals are heavily hunted for their fur. But there are still about 5 million of these seals in the world.*

Overleaf. *The spotted seal* (Phoca largha) *of the Bering Sea is closely related to the harbor seal, but has become totally dependent on sea ice for the rearing of young, whereas the harbor seal rears its young on shore.*

Above. *In a grotesque display that may warn other males not to encroach on his territory, a male hooded seal inflates the rubbery septum between the nasal passages and extrudes the septum from his nose. This "balloon" may be extruded alternately from the two nostrils while the seal shakes its head up and down.*

162. *The hood-like proboscis of the male hooded seal becomes inflated when the animal is alarmed or agitated. Females lack an expandable proboscis. Males may weigh as much as 400 kilograms; females are about half that size.*

occasionally use land to haul out on. Other marine mammals, such as the hair seals (Phocidae) of the Arctic and Antarctic, rarely use land at all, using sea ice for resting, bearing young, and nursing. Whales, just as seals, have adapted to the sea, but do not use land or sea ice for any direct purpose, except perhaps as shelter. Sea ice, formed from seawater and occurring hundreds of kilometers from land, is a part of the sea, and those animals that use it for hauling out or for shelter can rightfully be classed as being totally marine. There is but one bird that never comes ashore, the emperor penguin; it breeds on fast ice close to the shore and can be considered as marine as the ice-inhabiting seals, walruses, and whales.

Sea ice has profound importance for seals and walruses, and a few species of whales. It dominates their lives all year long and is a major determinant of their social structure. There are four species of ice-inhabiting Antarctic seals—Weddell, crabeater, Ross, and leopard—and six in the Arctic—ring, ribbon, bearded, spotted, harp, and hooded. All belong to the hair seal family, and are quite different from the sea lions and fur seals of the family Otariidae, which have little, pointed, external ears. Using all four limbs, members of Otariidae can run and walk on land rather well. The phocids lack external ears, possessing only a little hole on each side of the head as a tell-tale sign of their very fine sense of hearing. They are spindle-shaped in body form and have lost the ability to turn their rear legs forward to aid in walking on land. They swim by means of side to side sweeps of their rear flippers, or progress over solid surfaces by hunching forward in caterpillar-like fashion. Not all of them, however, are slow on icy surfaces; the crabeater and ribbon seals and some others can "swim," reptile-like, over smooth sea ice at a pace equal to a man at full trot. Nevertheless, this very limited locomotor ability out of the water inhibits their ability to flee from land predators. In the Antarctic there are no land predators, so seals there are almost totally unafraid of a person approaching them on the ice. But in the Arctic, the polar bear stalks, Eskimos hunt, and wolves, bears, and foxes patrol the beaches; thus, the seals there are exceedingly wary and difficult to approach.

The one species of walrus, which inhabits only boreal and Arctic seas, is like a cross between seals and sea lions. It has no external ears, but it can walk, albeit clumsily, on land or sea ice with the aid of its rear flippers. In the water it swims like a hair seal most of the time, but occasionally uses its front flippers as sea lions do, swimming by flapping them much as if it had wings. For the walrus and the 10 seals that are ice-inhabiting, sea ice is actively sought as a place to rest. Most whales, on the other hand, avoid heavy ice; only three types of whales live in icy waters all year—the bowhead whale, narwhal, and the belukha. Others such as the rorquals (the giant blue whale and its relatives) may inhabit sea ice dominated waters a good portion of the year, but do not inhabit them continuously. Though the latter seek polar seas to feed, their adaptation to ice is not as complete as that of the bowhead whale which never leaves a sea ice habitat.

Sea ice plays an important role in all phases of marine

A male ribbon seal (Histriophoca fasciata) *rests on sea ice off Seward Peninsula in the Bering Sea. This species is found in the northern Pacific from Sakhalin Island well into the Arctic. In summer, it leaves the sea ice and becomes pelagic.*

Above. *Crabeater seals* (Lobodon carcinophagus) *are the most numerous pinnipeds. More than 15 million of these animals inhabit the sea ice of the Southern Ocean. The seal does not feed on crabs, as its name suggests, but on the abundant krill found in Antarctic waters.*

Left. *A Weddell seal pup has hauled out on Antarctic sea ice. Weddell seals stretch out perpendicular to the sun, as do lizards, to receive maximum solar radiation in spring and summer.*

Overleaf. *The Antarctic leopard seal* (Hydrurga leptonyx), *named for its spotted coat, is ubiquitous in the Southern Ocean. Although this seal is best known for its habit of eating penguins, it feeds primarily on fish.*

mammal life history. The ice-inhabiting seals and the walruses, unlike whales, must haul out to rest, breed, and nurse. Each of these species has generally become adapted not only to different foods, but also to different sorts of sea ice, each evolving its own peculiar social structure as a consequence. Some, such as walruses and Weddell seals, are highly gregarious and are found lying together in large herds. Some, such as bearded seals, are solitary and territorial, apportioning ice territories to be defended. Others form breeding pairs and use ice as a platform for mating purposes, and still others have combinations of these life styles.

Social Life of the Walrus

What we know of marine mammals derives mostly from what we see of them at the surface of the sea. Studying their social lives has been likened to looking at an iceberg; we see only the very tip. We have not yet developed an equivalent of bird watching—seal watching under water —and can only gain hints of what goes on below.

What we know of walruses exemplifies this fact. Walruses are highly social and gregarious at all times of the year. Further, they almost compulsively make body contact with their neighbors. This contrasts with the many social seals which gather together but generally avoid body contact. A herd of walruses looks like a continuous brown mass, but the social structure of the herd is a sophisticated set of hierarchies in which social dominance is apparently well established among males, females, and the young.

It appears that walruses not only organize themselves into social hierarchies within the herd, but also form segregated groups of individuals which may be functioning quite independently. Herds of females, associated with immature animals, calves, and a few mature males, aggregate on sea ice in May of each year. There may be subgroups of pregnant, near-term females, somewhat apart from the larger group. All subgroups together may number from a few tens of individuals to thousands.

As calves are born and the ice pack recedes northward, melting under spring and summer sun, the entire herd moves northward. Meanwhile, other herds, composed largely of males, may also move north with the ice, quite apart from the females, but only some of the males move into the Chukchi Sea to the same northern ice as the females and young. Many males separate from the main herd and haul out on various islands on both the United States and Russian sides of Beringia. There, on dry land, they are relatively easy to observe.

Male walruses establish social dominance among themselves according to tusk and body size: the larger the animal and the longer its tusks, the more dominant it is among other males. Thus a hierarchy is set up, much like the well-known pecking order among chickens. This is very convenient because indicators such as body size and tusk length usually replace the need to fight and risk injury. Fighting does occur among males, as the scars about the neck indicate, but a male which displays its long tusks rarely has to fight another animal with shorter tusks. Female walruses also have tusks, but studies have not yet been done to determine whether or not they too establish hierarchies; casual observations indicate that they do. The advancing ice of fall and early winter forces the males to desert their summering areas. They meet the female herds—forced south by advancing ice—in the central and southern Bering Sea by January. Both males and females are then coming into reproductive condition. Walruses are one of the latest-maturing of all mammals; females may not bear their first calf until age 10 and males usually do not father a calf until age 15. And females must nurse their calf for almost 2 years; thus, they bear a new calf only every second or third year. By late January, the extraordinary courtship (described later in this chapter) of the walruses has begun. The herds have congregated on heavy ice at least a meter in thickness and well behind the front where sea ice is stable and protected from the undulating movements of the ocean. They especially like areas where the heavy ice has been broken into large floes separated by river-like leads. About a third of the females are impregnated at this time, and another third will soon bear young, having mated the year before. The final third remains non-productive.

No one has ever observed the birth of a walrus and recorded it. Judging from the process in seals, the birth is probably rapid. No doubt the young and mother exchange vocal expressions—soft grunts from the female and expressive "ooks" from the calf. And probably they also "exchange-breathe," placing their muzzles close to each other and breathing in and out. Thus, they soon get to know each other. The calf has little blubber, weighing only 50 to 70 kilograms when born. Its color is soft gray. It can swim, though only weakly.

After birth the calf does not enter the water. It stays on the ice with its mother, keeping on her lee side. This usually turns out to be the belly side of the mother, where four teats yield a milk richer than cow's cream. The milk is about 35 percent butterfat, 6 percent protein, and contains no sugar. The calf takes food briefly but often, perhaps 6 to 10 times a day, judging from the behavior of captives. Soon, the frequency of nursing decreases, but the quantity consumed at each nursing increases. The calf possibly consumes over a tenth of its body weight a day— costing the mother twice that weight in her own bulk— until the calf can swim, at which time the mother can again feed. Even with this tremendous food consumption, growth is not nearly as rapid as it is in seals. The calf most often stays with the mother, nursing less and less frequently for almost 2 years, gaining protection, warmth, and guidance. The calf swims often and strongly by the end of its first month, having accumulated enough blubber to protect it from the extreme cold.

The first months of the calf's life are usually not difficult. Weather is mild, even in the far north of the Chukchi Sea where the female-dominated herds congregate. The sun is high, and the ice is in retreat. But in early September, the sea again begins to freeze. The herds must move south well ahead of the advancing ice. By fall, the calf can dive well enough to feed on clams and other benthic invertebrates. It needs all the strength it can muster, for the retreat south often involves days of swimming in icy water. By the end of its first year of life it is strong and well over 200 kilograms in weight. During this first year a baby walrus has probably consumed well over 2,000 liters

Sailing south with the currents, an Arctic iceberg that probably originated in Greenland or Ellesmere Island floats in the waters of Notre Dame Bay, Newfoundland.

172–173. *Melting or decaying icebergs of the Antarctic may have fantastic shapes. Some of the icebergs have sheer ice palisades; others have frozen towers and spires. The distinguishing feature of newly created Antarctic icebergs is their tabular shape. Although these icebergs may be up to 600 meters thick, they are flat on top because they have broken from the ice shelf that surrounds the frozen mainland. There are few ice shelves in the Arctic; icebergs there originate from calving glaciers that break into irregular, relatively small shapes. Icebergs of Antarctica, on the other hand, may be the size of the state of Rhode Island. Early explorers of the polar seas sometimes mistook icebergs for new lands.*

Overleaf. *Amidst floating ice chunks, walruses (Odobenus rosmarus) display their wrinkled, bewhiskered faces and ivory tusks. The hide of the male walrus is as thick as a man's thumb in general, with the hide of the neck reaching 7 centimeters in thickness. In females the hide is uniformly about 1 centimeter thick. Beneath the hide is a layer of blubber 10 centimeters thick.*

The tusks, which in male walruses may grow a meter long, are used to help determine dominance among males and, occasionally, to aid the animal in pulling itself out of the water. Contrary to popular belief, the walrus does not use the tusks to dig out shellfish on the bottom. But it does use its facial whiskers to locate food on the bottom.

of milk and has eaten more than a ton of clams and other invertebrates.

Songs Beneath the Sea

One of the best known of all marine mammals in terms of its behavior in the wild—both above water and below—is the Weddell seal of the Antarctic. This is a very placid beast, allowing close approach and rarely trying to bite unless hard pressed. Its habitat in shorefast ice means that some populations are easily accessible from Antarctic research stations. One can dive with these seals and observe them under the ice, too. In the mid-1960's, underwater observations of Weddell seals under the ice showed that both males and females near their rookeries produce many sounds, including a trill—much like the prolonged chirping of a mechanical canary—which descends to a series of "chugs." This sound is evidently produced only during the spring breeding season. Furthermore, when seals produce the trills, other seals seem to take notice. Since they appear to trill mostly near breathing holes in the ice, it was proposed that the seals "sing" to defend their breathing hole territory. It may be that when the males trill, they are protecting a breeding territory and when females do so, they are protecting the area of ice around their pups. It also appears that there are not enough breathing holes to go around for the entire population. Thus, the song announces to other seals, "This is my area."

No one has ever seen a wild male walrus sing underwater, but by means of an underwater microphone, called a hydrophone, we can hear them. And what a song it is! It begins with two taps, close together, followed by a bell sound—"tap-tap-bo . . . ing . . . g . . . g . . . g." There may be up to four of these sequences, then a long series of taps followed by a coda, almost exactly the pattern of "shave-and-a-haircut-two-bits!" More taps follow, and perhaps another "bo . . . ing . . . g . . . g . . . g," and the animal emerges with a brief, mellow whistle made between its beefsteak-sized lips. This goes on and on, but how the females respond is hard to tell, for no one has ever seen mating. The song, which travels several kilometers underwater, may serve to establish territories or spacing among males and to communicate their breeding condition to females.

The bearded seal (*Erignathus barbatus*) of the Arctic is another singing seal. This species inhabits fairly dense pack ice. In the springtime, a hydrophone may pick up strong descending trills somewhat reminiscent of those of the Weddell seal, except that they are even more musical, and even frequency-modulated, that is, one wavering trill is superimposed upon another.

Seals and walruses are not the only polar marine mammals which make sounds underwater. The white whale, or belukha (*Delphinapterus leucas*) is nicknamed "sea canary" because it is so musically loquacious. The narwhal (*Monodon monoceros*) makes strange creaking noises. The bowhead whale (*Balaena mysticetus*) groans in low tones. And herds of harp seals (*Pagophilus groenlandicus*) sound like a whole barnyard full of pigs and chickens when they gather in the spring to reproduce and bear young. Sound is evidently an effective way to communicate and apportion space in the polar seas.

Above. *Walruses break holes in the ice for breathing. They often sleep in the water, with only their heads above the surface.*

Overleaf. *A band of walruses clusters on ice floes in the Chukchi Sea. Walruses usually ride floating ice as it drifts north in spring, but in autumn they swim south ahead of the freezing ice. These gregarious animals sometimes gather in herds of hundreds or even thousands of individuals.*

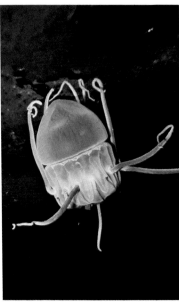

It travels five times faster in water than in air, over a kilometer-and-a-half a second. It also travels farther. It has been calculated that many marine mammals can communicate over distances of 10 or 20 kilometers. Hence, individuals of a herd may occupy 300 square kilometers and still remain in contact. It is even theoretically possible that some larger baleen whales, which produce very low frequency sounds, can communicate over 100 kilometers distance because low frequency sounds can travel much farther than higher frequency ones. This may enable these whales to sing or maintain social contact over an area of 30,000 square kilometers! But of course this is highly conjectural.

Lives of Whales

The bowhead may be the most unusual of all the baleen whales, for it inhabits polar waters year round and does not migrate to warmer water as other baleen whales do. Bowheads occur in waters of the Canadian Archipelago and near Greenland, but are most common in the waters of Beringia. Bowhead numbers are not known for sure, but populations probably do not exceed a tenth of their former abundance. Giving any population figure is a highly uncertain business for no one has yet determined how to count whales with much greater than 50 percent accuracy! In winter, the Beringian bowhead population is spread out in the waters of the central Bering Sea where there is heavy ice, but not so heavy as to prevent their surfacing to breathe. The bowhead is aided in this respect by an elevation on its head in which the blowholes, or nostrils, are placed. With this projection, bowheads can break ice a half meter or more in thickness. A mere crack in the ice or a narrow lead between floes is all the bowhead needs to take a breath of air, its surfacing betrayed only by the appearance of a sudden V-shaped double spout of condensed breath. The spout dissipates soon after the bowhead inhales fresh air and descends below the ice. The bowheads begin their migration in spring, gathering in small groups and staying in fairly heavy ice. They are well ahead of the walruses and seals, passing through the Bering Strait in May while the walruses may pass by a couple of weeks later and some seals only after mid-June. By mid-May the bowheads are well into the Chukchi Sea, entering the Beaufort Sea in June and reaching their summer feeding grounds in the eastern Beaufort Sea, or near the ice front of the Chukchi, by July. Most of them migrate largely within a rift in the ice called the flaw or sheer zone, which occurs between the shore ice and the offshore ice—at least that is the hypothesis. When whaling for Beringian bowheads was at its peak a hundred years ago, catches in summer were heavy all along the summer ice front.

Bowhead food has not yet been precisely determined, but copepods are probably the most important. These are much smaller crustaceans than krill, but the bowhead can filter them out from water with its very fine baleen. But a major question is: How does the bowhead maintain its population in the supposedly low productivity areas it inhabits? Attesting to the low productivity of the Beaufort Sea waters, which this whale inhabits in summer, is the fact that only one seal, the little ringed seal (*Phoca hispida*), and only one whale, the belukha, are abundant

180 top. *A comb jelly (Order Cydippida) floats in the water of Resolute Bay, Northwest Territories. These filter feeders catch food using their comb-like cilia, which create currents that direct plankton toward their mouths.*

Bottom. *The jellyfish Periphylla of Antarctic waters belongs to a group of coronate jellyfishes that live in deep water in many parts of the world.*

Opposite. *The icefish (Pagetopsis macropterus) of the Southern Ocean is a member of the only vertebrate family with colorless blood; this is due to an absence of red blood cells.*

Above. *A belukha, or white whale*
(Delphinapterus leucas), *surfaces
in the Canadian Arctic. This
whale is a coastal species that
hunts fish, squid, and
invertebrates, which it often
pursues into harbors and rivers.
The belukha is a highly
maneuverable animal in the
water; it is even able to swim
backward by sculling with its
flukes.*

Left. *A school of white whales travels through cold Canadian waters. Belukhas often are seen in very large groups, sometimes numbering hundreds of animals. These groups, however, do not represent well defined social units, but are random assemblages of ten or fewer whales. White whales are very vocal and, because of the many sounds they emit under water, are known as "sea canaries."*

there. Perhaps the whales are just more efficient in their feeding than most other marine mammals. Or perhaps we are trying, incorrectly, to relate what we know of other baleen whales to the bowhead. Most baleen whales concentrate their eating in the summertime, fasting or eating sparsely at other times of the year. Perhaps the bowhead is able to feed all year round, exploiting unidentified food sources. Thus, it may also find food in winter in the Bering Sea at a time when other large whales supposedly eat little.

The bowhead's time of copulation is also odd. It may mate in summer, rather than in late fall or winter, when the other baleen whales perform this function.

All in all, the bowhead may be the most remarkable of the baleen whales, for it is a marked exception to "rules" of the others. It does not migrate to warm waters like the rorquals, for example, the blue whale (*Balaenoptera musculus*), which reaches a length of over 30 meters, and the fin (*Balaenoptera physalus*), which may reach over 20 meters in length. These rorquals feed in polar and subpolar seas, but then travel to temperate and even tropical seas where they bear their young. Another kind of baleen whale, the gray whale (*Eschrichtius robustus*), is also found in Arctic seas only during summer. It winters in warm tropical lagoons of Mexico where its calves are born and nursed. The right whale (*Eubalaena glacialis*), the nearest relative of the bowhead, is really a coastal, temperate species which enters subpolar seas only marginally and is now exceedingly rare, except off South Africa where it is making a strong comeback.

The narwhal and the belukha are closely related inhabitants of ice-dominated waters. Both are toothed whales, but the adult narwhal has no teeth in the jaws. Instead, one incisor projects through its upper jaw to produce a twisted tusk with a left hand thread. Usually only one tusk pokes out, extending as much as 2½ meters. Occasionally there are two tusks. And here rests one of the strangest violations of a biological rule of nature. All vertebrate animals are supposed to exhibit bilateral symmetry, meaning that one side of the body is a mirror image of the other. But in the narwhal's case, if there are two tusks, both have a left hand thread. That is a bit like having two left hands. As for the use of this tusk, recent research appears to confirm the expected. The tusk is found only on males, and is apparently used mostly for sexual display, and only occasionally for fighting. This is analogous to the antlers of a deer. Males have been seen displaying the tusks, and even crossing them above the water's surface like gladiators. Are they, like the walrus, setting up their own hierarchies by means of this display?

The belukha, or white whale, is much better known. It is not so wedded to an ice habitat as the bowhead or narwhal. It is found as far south as Canada's St. Lawrence River and southern Alaska. Calves are born a slate color, turning white by the time they are mature. They are mostly fish-eaters, but they also consume a variety of invertebrates. They are known to follow salmon up rivers, riding the tides and consuming these economically valuable fishes. When salmon and belukhas were abundant and fishermen were not, days long past, such feeding practices did not interfere with anyone's livelihood. But this feeding habit of the belukha has recently resulted in a

Near open water of the Canadian Arctic, a Minke whale (Balaenoptera acutorostrata) *surfaces to breathe through a small hole. This is the only rorqual whale that inhabits loose ice throughout the year; the Minke is too small—only 10 meters long—to break through heavy ice.*

conflict with the fishermen. As few wish to kill these beautiful and docile creatures, a partial solution to this conflict between whales and fishermen has been to play the recorded sounds of the killer whale (*Orcinus orca*) underwater where the belukhas congregate, causing them to flee and leave the fish to the fishermen.

The killer whale also inhabits polar waters. It is the largest of the dolphins, the largest males reaching about 8 meters in length and attaining a weight of from 5 to 6 tons. It is found in temperate seas, but seems to be most abundant in the Southern Ocean and the North Pacific, north into Beringia. It is beautifully marked, with splashes of white above the eye, under the dorsal fin, and on the belly. Truly a "killer," it can kill the largest whales, as well as seals, dolphins, and sea lions, but fish form the bulk of its diet. It attacks large baleen whales in wolf-like groups, eating out the tongue of its prey, stripping off the blubber, and taking out huge chunks of flesh. It is also capable of eating small seals whole. On the other hand, in captivity it has demonstrated a keen intelligence and a great gentleness.

A "Terrestrial" Marine Mammal

To illustrate how generalities about nature are always ripe for violation, consider the polar bear. It is twice the weight of a tiger and at least as large as the Alaska brown bear. It is relatively fearless of humans, and may even attack. But mostly it just ignores us.

The polar bear evolved from a grizzly-like ancestor during the Ice Age. It is a marine mammal only by virtue of the fact that it is most at home roaming sea ice and searching for a diet of seals and young, vulnerable walruses; it is not particularly modified anatomically or physiologically for an aquatic life. Nevertheless, most of the polar bear's food consists of marine mammals. It occasionally takes fish, but preys mostly on those marine species that inhabit the sea ice and fail to make a quick exit at the approach of the bear. It is able to search out the pupping dens of ringed seals among the confused piles of broken shorefast ice. It can then dig out and eat the pups. At other times of the year, it will wait near a breathing hole, in the ice, of an adult ringed seal. When the seal surfaces, the polar bear scoops it from the water with one swipe of its powerful clawed front foot. The ringed seal has been considered the major item of diet of the polar bear, but this is in part because polar bears have been observed mostly near shore where ringed seals predominate and where scientists can best observe them.

Polar bears are abundant far out to sea, inhabiting sea ice hundreds of miles from shore. As few ringed seals are found so far from shorefast ice, one wonders what the polar bear subsists on there. Walruses are the largest of all northern seal-like creatures. Existing where they do and in large herds, one would not think that the walrus would fear the polar bear, for how could a bear attack such a huge and powerfully tusked animal? Nevertheless, walruses are fearful when hauled out on ice—unlike seals of the Antarctic, where no large, terrestrial predator exists. Walruses panic when approached on the ice by humans or bears, and in their rush into the water, a calf is often the last one in. A polar bear will actually charge a walrus group, seemingly so that it will panic. It may be

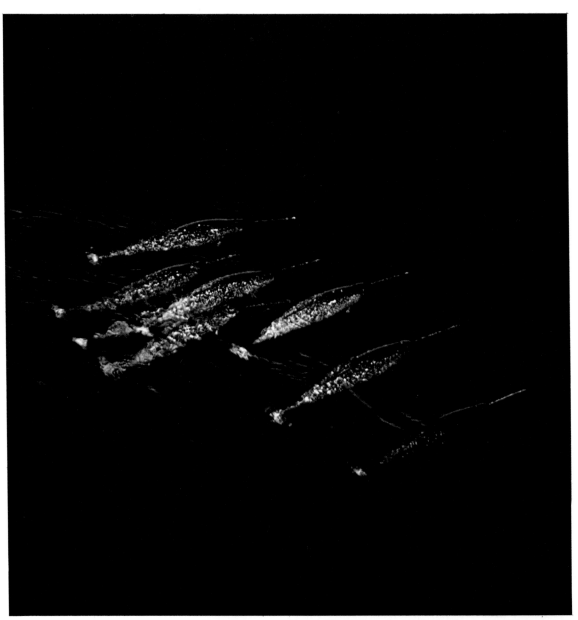

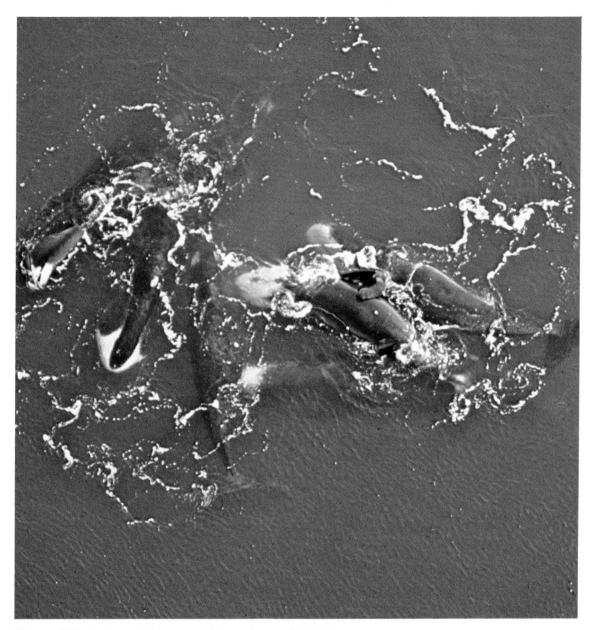

186 top. *With tusks reminiscent of those of the mythical unicorn, male narwhals* (Monodon monoceros) *swim through Barrow Strait in the Canadian Arctic. The tusks, present only in males, are used for display, probably for determining social dominance.*

Bottom. *A blue whale* (Balaenoptera musculus) *exhales as it surfaces. The spout that rises from the whale's blowhole is the result of condensing water vapor from the warm air in the whale's lungs. The blue whale is the largest animal that has ever existed.*

Above. *Surrounded by its companions, a pair of bowhead whales* (Balaena mysticetus) *mates near the surface in the southern Beaufort Sea. Breeding occurs in late summer; calves are born about a year later. Once hunted almost to extinction, bowheads now number possibly 2,000 to 3,000 individuals.*

lucky enough to grasp a youngster by the rear flippers before it enters the water. After killing the little walrus, the bear makes an incision behind the head and proceeds to eat away the blubber and flesh so that, eventually, the skin of the walrus is turned inside out and is all that remains except for bones.

Our Relatives in the Sea

Seals and whales are mammals, yet they can stay warm in polar seas, dive thousands of meters below the surface —at least a kilometer or two—and stay there for over an hour. They can do this because they are able to tolerate great blood acidity, produced by the accumulation of metabolic by-products, and because they can store greater amounts of oxygen than we can. Their thermoregulation, or the control of heat intake and output, is a sophisticated blend of body size and shape, insulation, heat exchangers in the flukes and flippers, vascular control of blood flow, and behavior. For them, the sea is warm, even the polar seas, provided all of their mechanisms are well adjusted; but should something go wrong, they may become vulnerable and die. Should, for example, their food supply fail and not enough blubber accumulate about their bodies, they could neither fend off cold nor produce enough heat to live. Pup seals, born too late in the season to nurse long enough, may be weaned too young and thin, and perish before the last of summer.

Somehow, possibly because they are most like us, the marine mammals seem most extraordinary, surviving—thriving!—in the most hostile place on Earth, the polar seas.

Opposite. A polar bear (Ursus maritimus) scavenges the carcass of a whale on the summer-warmed coasts of Alaska's William O. Douglas Arctic Wildlife Range. Like other animals that live in cold climates, the polar bear has considerable fat, which provides energy and insulation.

Above. *The fur of the polar bear is thick and densely packed, providing effective insulation in water as well as on land.*

Overleaf. *A lone male polar bear treks across the ice of northern Hudson Bay. During winter, polar bears move south along the shores of the bay. Near the shore, polar bears prey primarily on ringed seals* (Phoca hispida) *that raise their pups in dens in pressure ridges of shorefast ice.*

Picture Credits

Numbers correspond to page numbers.

Appendix

Landforms of the Polar Regions

Glaciers

Glaciers, permanent bodies of snow and ice, play a dominant role in shaping the major landforms at high latitudes. They occur in all sizes, from the small cirque glaciers forming amphitheater-shaped bowls among mountains to the huge ice masses of continental size covering most of Greenland and the Antarctic. The Greenland Ice sheet covers 1.7 million square kilometers and is as much as 1,000 meters thick in its center. But this continental glacier pales when compared with the Antarctic Ice Sheet, which encompasses some 11.5 million square kilometers and is 4,500 meters thick. Ninety percent of all the fresh water in the world is tied up in glaciers.

Eskers

Glaciers are not static blocks of ice; they advance or retreat as snow accumulates or thaws. As the glaciers advance, they grind away at the underlying substrate, plucking rocks and soil from the surface to be transported along with the ice. Some of this unsorted material may be deposited along the edge of the glaciers, while some is carried to the terminus. Other material is carried by meltwater streams flowing on or beneath glaciers and is deposited along their courses. After the glaciers melt, they leave moraines that can be recognized as long, sinuous ridges, known as eskers. Eskers are common in the Arctic and, because of their height, provide windbreaks and sheltered areas.

Ice-Scoured Plain

When large ice masses move over a broad area, they may erode the underlying surface to a relatively flat plain, leaving numerous shallow lakes where they have cut more deeply, and small hills where the rock is more resistant. Perhaps the best known of these ice-scoured plains is the Canadian Shield, which encompasses the eastern half of Canada, from the Maritime Provinces to Manitoba and Saskatchewan. Other broad plains are found in Scandinavian countries.

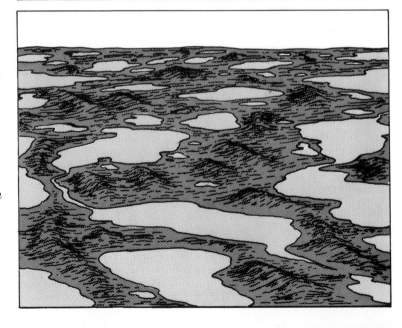

Glacial Striae

Glacial striae, a series of long, generally parallel gouges on the surface of the bedrock, are unquestionable evidence of the passage of an ice sheet. They form as the weight of the glacier polishes the bedrock, removing rough edges and abrading the surface. The alignment of the resulting striae can be used to determine the direction of glacial movement.

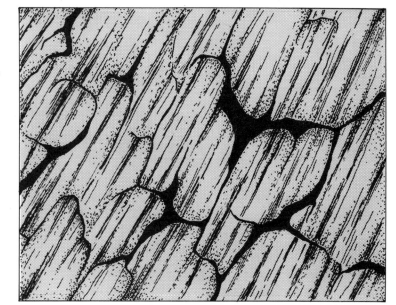

Felsenmeer

Frost action—the repeated cycle of freezing and thawing—is the most important cause of mechanical weathering in polar areas. As such, it is the major process in the formation of many small-scale geological features. The pressure exerted by the expansion of water when it freezes is sufficient to fracture rocks. In areas where large expanses of bedrock have been exposed by glaciers, frost action can be sufficient to split it into a sea of rock, or felsenmeer.

Stone Rings

In areas where the soil is underlain by a layer of permanently frozen earth, or permafrost, the pressure of freezing is exerted laterally and vertically. As a result, both coarse and fine particles are forced sideways and upward. When the ice melts, small materials can return to their original locations whereas the larger ones tend to remain in place. The repeated freezing cycle eventually sorts the materials, resulting in the formation of rings of stone that are often arranged in an extremely regular fashion. Rings up to 10 meters in diameter have been discovered.

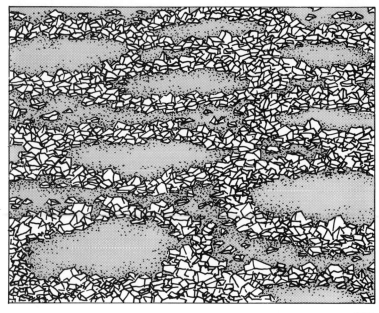

Life on the Continent

Chlamydomonas nivalis (.01 mm)

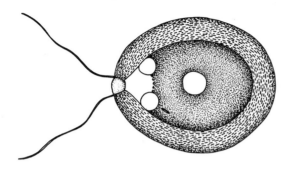

Usnea antarctica (7 cm)

Colobanthus crassifolius (3 cm)

Lichens are by far the most common form of Antarctic terrestrial life. Over 350 species have been found, and the diversity of the lichen assemblage is almost unparalleled. Most occur near the shores, but one has been reported as far inland as 86° south latitude, within 390 kilometers of the pole itself. These primitive plants are extremely hardy. Long-lived and able to tolerate long periods of drought, many survived on the continent during the height of the Pleistocene glaciation.

The typical crustose or foliose lichens found elsewhere in the world also occur in the polar regions. One fairly common species around the Antarctic Peninsula is the fruticose, or "shrubby" lichen (Usnea antarctica).

Algae are wide-spread, and at least five of the main algal groups have been discovered: blue-green, green, diatoms, golden-brown, and yellow-green. Some occur on rock surfaces, while others form thick mats on the bottoms of permanently ice-covered ponds. The snow algae are probably of the greatest interest to visitors, as they grow on the surface of the snow itself. Growth occurs where there is abundant sunshine and when the temperature of the snow is at the melting point.

Chlamydomonas nivalis, the most abundant snow alga, is a green alga. During the winter, it turns pinkish-red due to the presence of a pigment, hematochrome. Pink snow also occurs in the Arctic and alpine regions, and is due to the same or related species of alga.

Colobanthus crassifolius, a species of chickweed, and Deschampsia antarctica, a grass, are the only vascular plants in Antarctica. They are confined to the western coasts of the Antarctic Peninsula. Typically, they grow in small clumps on sunny slopes near seabird colonies within a few meters of the coast. These plants are true Antarctic natives, but their origins are obscure.

Though meager in species and distribution, the plant communities of the Antarctic provide habitats for arthropods, the only true terrestrial animals of the continent. Well over 100 species have been recorded, most from the Peninsula area. Nearly half of these do not maintain an independent existence but are parasitic upon birds, seals, or other arthropods.

Mites (Acarina) are by far the most common and widely distributed arthropods.

Cryptopygus antarcticus (2 mm)

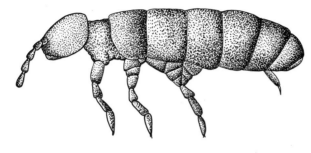

Nanorchestes antarcticus *has been found as far south as 85° south latitude, which makes it the southernmost animal in the world, if we ignore the occasional seabird that may overfly the pole. Dessication is the most severe hazard to arthropods, so* N. antarcticus, *like most other species, occurs mainly in the upper layer of the soil where the relative humidity is high. Ticks (Acarina), associated with bird colonies, and springtails (Collembola) are perhaps the arthropods most likely to be encountered by the casual observer. Largest of the springtails, Cryptopygus antarcticus feeds on detritus, found commonly among mosses or lichens or in other protected areas.*

Wingless insects are common on islands all over the world and it is not particularly surprising that the Antarctic has its own representative. Belgica antarctica (Diptera), a black midge 4 millimeters long, is the largest free-living invertebrate on the continent. Sometimes the adults form clusters of several hundred individuals. Its closest relatives are found in South America.

Few places in the world are free of fleas, and the Antarctic is no exception. However the single indigenous species, Glaciopsyllus antarcticus, is not a pest to humans or mammals, but is found only in the nests or on the bodies of some seabirds in east Antarctica.

Belgica antarctica (4 mm)

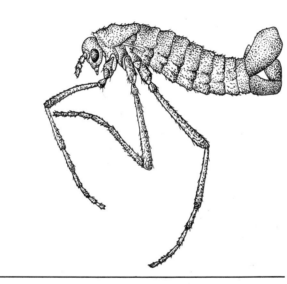

The origins of the Antarctic fauna and flora are still controversial. Certainly some of the plants and a few arthropods were present before the Pleistocene period, and were able to persist through the height of glaciation. Others are of more recent origin, perhaps carried to Antarctica by migratory birds, or transported by ocean currents. The wind is a powerful agent of dispersal, and this may explain the occasional appearance of spiders—and even a vagrant butterfly!

For the most part, human activity does not seem to have been responsible for the introduction of more than a few exotic plants and animals. An exception is Poa pratensis, *a grass native to Tierra del Fuego, which has been reported on the Antarctic Peninsula. Simple ecosystems, such as those in the Antarctic, are easily disrupted. Therefore, increasing scientific activity and, especially, tourist ships must be carefully controlled so that accidental introductions do not occur.*

Glaciopsyllus antarcticus (1 mm)

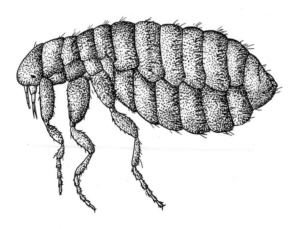

Antarctic Marine Algae

Charcotia actonichilus (×1000)

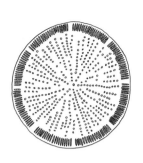

Rhizosolenia chunii (×1000)

Fragilariopsis kerguelensis (×1500)

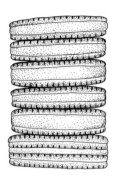

Chaetoceros neglectus (×500)

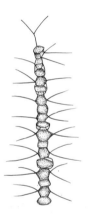

Chaetoceros criophilus (×500)

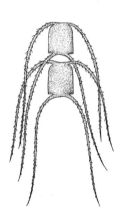

Gonyaulax sphaeroidea (×1000)

Two groups of planktonic microalgae predominate in Antarctic waters, the diatoms and the dinoflagellates. Diatoms consist of two parts that fit together like the top and bottom of a Petri plate. Diatoms are perforated with pores. Charcotia actinochilus has pores arranged symmetrically around a central point, while Rhizosolenia chunii is an elongated plant with many belt-like bands forming between the two plate-like ends. Another basic diatom type is boat-shaped, being symmetrical around a mid-plane rather than a midpoint. An example of this type is Fragilariopsis kerguelensis. Some diatoms produce long, hair-like extensions, like the genus Chaetoceros. Its cells form chains, and the spines produced from each cell wind around those of the adjacent cell. These

extensions are thought to influence the way a cell or a filament of cells sinks through the water. In seas of warmer, less dense water, the spines are long and often branched; in polar regions they are shorter. Dinoflagellates are unicellular plants characterized by plates of cellulose arranged in characteristic patterns, and by spines and horns that extend out from the cells. The Antarctic genus Podolampas has a well-developed horn at the apex and two at the opposite side. Others are more rounded in shape, like Gonyaulax sphaeroidea, redrawn here from an electron micrograph, which shows the conspicuous pores, plates, and furrows. These organisms are able to swim, propelling themselves with two tiny hair-like filaments called flagella—one

that wraps around the cell and lies within a girdle around the middle, and a second that extends along a furrow and out below the cell between the two horns opposing the apex.

The largest and most conspicuous of the Antarctic macroalgae are brown algae. Only one, Cystosphaera jacquinotii, has floats—round, pod-like structures, that provide support in the water. This is a very large alga that occurs only along the Antarctic Peninsula. It is held to the bottom by a root-like attachment called a holdfast, from which a single main stem, or stipe, arises and then divides to form alternately branched and flattened blades.

One of the largest Antarctic brown algae is the giant blade-forming Phyllogigas grandifolius, which can reach lengths of 15

Cystosphaera jacquinotii (37 cm)

Phyllogigas grandifolius (2.5 m)

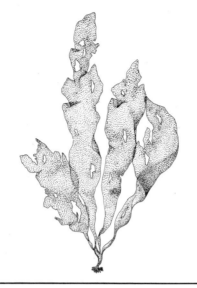

Desmarestia menziesii (35 cm)

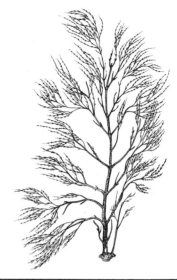

Leptosomia simplex (37 cm)

Plocamium secundatum (13 cm)

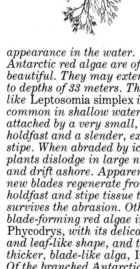

Iridaea obovata (20 cm)

meters. This plant, because of its variability in shape, has been the source of considerable confusion since it was first described in 1905. Only recently have adequate collections of both young and mature plants been available for study, so that the earliest developmental stages are now understood. The plant is related to the more highly branched Desmarestia, of which there are several Antarctic species. Among the most conspicuous Antarctic macroalgae are the bush-like Desmarestia *plants, of which* Desmarestia menziesii *is an abundant example. This plant has a rounded holdfast with a conspicuous collar from which projects a somewhat flattened stipe. A series of opposed branches forms along the stipe; these, in turn, are branched to produce an almost feathery*

appearance in the water. Antarctic red algae are often very beautiful. They may extend down to depths of 33 meters. The blade-like Leptosomia simplex *is common in shallow water, being attached by a very small, delicate holdfast and a slender, expanding stipe. When abraded by ice, these plants dislodge in large numbers and drift ashore. Apparently, new blades regenerate from the holdfast and stipe tissue that survives the abrasion. Other blade-forming red algae include* Phycodrys, *with its delicate veins and leaf-like shape, and the thicker, blade-like alga,* Iridaia. *Of the branched Antarctic red algae the most common is* Plocamium, *which forms a delicate series of branchlets along a narrow, flattened series of branches. Occasionally,* Plocamium *acts as a support for*

the growth of the leafy epiphytic alga Monostroma (*shown here*). *Ice-scour affects the distribution of all Antarctic algae. Its effects are most evident at 5- to 10-meter depths, and sometimes to depths as great as 25 meters. As one progresses south along the Antarctic Peninsula and along the coast of Victoria Land, macroalgal assemblages become less dense and less diverse, probably because of the longer period of ice cover, and severity of winter conditions. However it should be kept in mind that comparatively little is known about the macroalgae of Antarctica and that, with further exploration and more detailed study of the organisms themselves, there is still much to be learned.*

199

Antarctic Marine Invertebrates

Aerothyris joubini (3 cm)

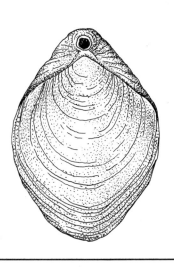

Arcoscalpellum gaussi (8 mm)

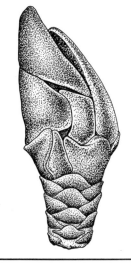

Promachocrinus kerguelensis (7 cm)

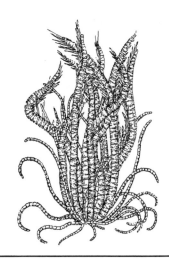

Gorgonocephalus (25 cm)

Lineus corrugatus (40 cm)

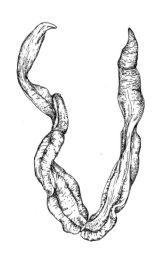

Odontaster (8 cm diameter)

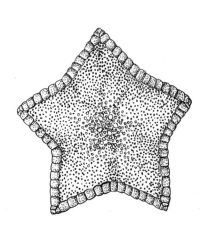

In the more than 30 million square kilometers of ocean that lie between the Antarctic convergence and Antarctica, there is an amazingly rich and diverse invertebrate fauna, both in the plankton and on the seafloor. The Antarctic marine invertebrate fauna has several unique features, most important being the high proportion of filter feeders on the seafloor, the high proportion of species found nowhere else, the high diversity and large numbers of some groups and the virtual absence of others, and the tendency in many groups toward greater parental care of the young than is seen elsewhere.

Near the Antarctic shore there is little permanent, well-developed shallow water invertebrate fauna. During the summer, a fauna of temporary residents, usually mobile foraging species, becomes established, but it is adversely affected by the scouring action of ice and by the formation of anchor ice. Below 20 meters and down to a depth of about 40 meters, a shallower zone is dominated by attached anemones and other coelenterates, and a deeper zone is dominated by sponges, bryozoans (sea mosses), and ascidians (sea squirts). The seafloor offers an ideal substrate for development of an assemblage of filter feeders, for it contains an abundance of gravels for attachment of organisms. Also, Antarctic bottom currents of 0.5 to 1 knot carry the abundant organic material to the feeding nets of the filter feeders.

Attached filter feeders dominate the benthic community; they include sponges in abundance, hydroids and other coelenterates, brachiopods (Aerothyris joubini), bryozoans, barnacles (Arcoscalpellum gaussi), and echinoderms, such as feather stars (Promachocrinus kerguelensis) and basket stars (Gorgonocephalus). Also present in large numbers are mobile scavengers such as polychaete worms and nemertean worms (Lineus corrugatus), crustaceans, and echinoderms such as starfish (Odontaster) and brittle stars (Amphiura). Mollusks are neither especially diverse nor especially common in the Antarctic. Among the crustaceans, notable absentees include the crabs and lobsters; the place usually occupied by these animals in the food web belongs to the large isopods (Acanthaspidia) and amphipods. Sea spiders (Austrodecus glaciale) are also common.

In most invertebrate groups,

Amphiura (10 cm diameter)

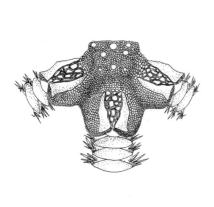

Acanthaspidia (20 mm)

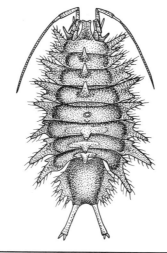

Austrodecus glaciale (15 mm)

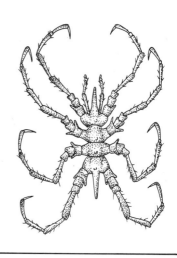

Leptychaster kerguelenensis (15 cm)

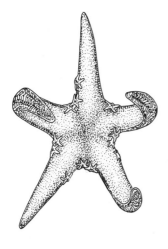

Abatus cordatus (5 cm)

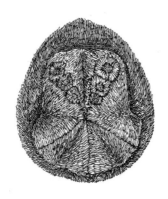

Psolus koehleri (65 cm)

approximately 70 percent of the species are restricted to the area south of the Antarctic convergence and are unknown elsewhere. Within that area, however, they may have a wide distribution, and many are circumpolar. The species that occur elsewhere in the world's oceans are almost invariably restricted to deeper water, where the temperature is always near freezing.

Another notable characteristic of the Antarctic marine invertebrate fauna is the presence of immense numbers of individuals. The seafloor can be carpeted with a crowded mass of filter feeders; many can be found clinging to the stems and branches of other animals and plants in order to gain access to clear feeding areas. The mobile organisms on the seafloor can also reach high population densities; as many as 14,000 small crustaceans can be found in an area of 1 square meter.

In warmer waters, most invertebrates reproduce by shedding eggs and sperm into the surrounding seawater. The young develop first as planktonic larvae, feeding on the plankton for several days or weeks and then, as juveniles, sink to the seafloor. In cold Antarctic waters, some species reproduce in the same "indirect" way. However, in at least 1,000 Antarctic species, "direct" development, in which the planktonic larval stage is reduced or eliminated, is the rule. In direct development, large, yolky eggs are produced, and the developing animal feeds upon this yolk material as it grows. Embryos and juveniles are often maintained in or on the body of the mother, as in the sea star (Leptychaster kerguelensis). In some groups, especially the sea urchins (Abatus cordatus) and sea cucumbers (Psolus koehleri), the mother has specially developed brood pouches for the rearing of the young. In P. koehleri, they are located just behind the feeding tentacles. This type of parental care ensures a high survival rate for the young.

Branta bernicla (62 cm)

Clangula hyemalis (56 cm)

Stercorarius pomarinus (56 cm)

Spring arrives in the northland with astonishing swiftness. The first sign of open water signals the arrival of eiders, loons, auks, and gulls. Shorebirds and cranes appear as soon as the marshes begin to thaw. Soon afterward, landbirds begin to sing from snow-free hillocks. The earliest arrivals may be driven back south by late storms, but they soon return. The migrants begin nesting as soon as possible, for the Arctic summer is short. The young must hatch by the time the first flush of insects occurs, and they must be ready to migrate before the first snows. Some species will move only as far south as the coniferous forest. Others, notably shorebirds, will undergo migrations that take them to Australia and Tierra del Fuego.

The brant (Branta bernicla) winters along temperate coasts, feeding on marine plants. By late spring, it is on the move toward nesting areas in the highest Arctic. These birds mate for life and return annually to the same familiar nesting area. Some pairs even mate before arrival, and the female begins laying almost immediately after reaching the site. Eggs are laid in mid-June and hatch in early July. Adults lead the goslings to open areas and freshwater ponds, where they are safe from predators, and then undergo a molt that renders them flightless for several weeks. By mid-August, the birds are in fresh plumage and ready for a long migration. When spring arrives late, the birds may not have time to raise a brood, in which case they forego breeding.

The oldsquaw, or long-tailed duck (Clangula hyemalis), is the most common of Arctic ducks. Except when nesting near freshwater ponds, the oldsquaw spends the year on the open ocean and in bays. Oldsquaws often nest within colonies of Arctic terns, behavior that affords protection from predators, as the terns are fierce in defense of their nests when danger approaches. The ducks remain paired only for a brief period. After the eggs are laid, the male moves back to the coasts, leaving the incubation and care of the young to the female.

Jaegers are hawklike birds of the oceans that are related to gulls. All of the three species nest only in the Arctic and are known for their predatory habits. The largest is the pomarine jaeger (Stercorarius pomarinus), a dark, falcon-like bird with a pair of twisted feathers projecting beyond the rest of the tail. Recent studies

Gavia stellata (66 cm)

Plectrophenax nivalis (17 cm)

Calidris alba (20 cm)

have shown that this species is highly nomadic and breeds only in areas where lemmings, its main source of food, occur. Thus, individuals may breed only two years in four.

Stout, dagger-like bills indicate the fish-eating habits of the loons. These ancient waterbirds are found only in the Northern Hemisphere. They are strong divers and use their large feet for underwater propulsion. The legs of the loon are set so far back on the body that the birds are nearly helpless on land and must build their flimsy nests on the shores of small lakes. Chicks are often ferried on the back of adults, providing them a warm and secure "island" for resting. Red-throated loons (Gavia stellata), Arctic loons (G. arctica), and yellow-billed loons (G. adamsii) all reach the high Arctic.

Though the Arctic region is rich in waterbirds, songbirds are not as well-represented. However, two common species are the Lapland longspur (Calcarius lapponicus) and snow bunting (Plectrophenax nivalis). Both species are finches and are primarily adapted for feeding on seeds; however, they consume large numbers of insects in summer when feeding their young. The average clutch size of Arctic songbirds is usually larger than that of the same or related species in temperate and tropical areas.

Sanderlings (Calidris alba) arrive at their breeding area in early June, and the male immediately performs a flight song. Given at low altitudes, as he sweeps back and forth over the tundra, the song establishes his territorial claim and announces his readiness to mate. Shorebirds typically lay a clutch of four eggs and, unlike the songbirds, do not show any latitudinal increase in clutch size. Yet the sanderling has found a way to effectively double its productivity. The female lays two clutches, each of four eggs. The first is brooded by the male and the second by the female, with each parent solely responsible for the care of its separate brood. In this way, sanderlings cope with the vagaries of the Arctic climate and take maximum advantage of years when conditions for breeding are most auspicious.

Resident Birds of the Arctic

Nyctea scandiaca (60 cm)

Falco rusticollis (56 cm)

Corvus corax (60 cm)

Very few birds possess adaptations that permit them to live in the Arctic year-round. Among them is the snowy owl (Nyctaea scandiaca). *Pure white with scattered black flecks, it is a creature of the tundra, where it feeds on small birds, ptarmigans, and lemmings. It lays a clutch of four to eight eggs and, like other owls, begins incubating with the first egg. As a result, the young are hatched on different days. When food is scarce, the oldest and largest will compete against the smaller chicks, which may then succumb. These birds often hunt by day, and are most likely to occur in open areas, such as lake shores or dunes along the ocean.*

The common raven (Corvus corax) *is one of the most adaptable of all birds. It is a permanent resident wherever it lives, from arid deserts to the high Arctic. During the Arctic winter, ravens survive as scavengers, often feeding on the carcasses or droppings of large mammals or foraging at garbage dumps. In summer, they prey on rodents and on the eggs and young of ducks and shorebirds. Canny birds, they often hunt in pairs; one flies far in the lead, waiting to be chased by an incubating shorebird, while the one in the rear locates the nest and steals the eggs.*

The ivory gull (Pagophila eburnea) *spends its entire life in the northernmost regions of the Arctic, always on or near drift ice. Pure white, with short black legs, it breeds in small colonies on Arctic islands. Its nest is a huge pile of moss and seaweed, which evidently insulates the eggs and young. A scavenger, the ivory gull follows polar bears and feeds, to a large extent, on their droppings and the remains of their prey. The webbing between the toes is much reduced compared to that found in other gulls, an adaptation that lessens the amount of heat lost to the ice or chilly water, and its claws are stout and curved to give it a secure grip on the ice.*

The rock ptarmigan (Lagopus mutus) *is the grouse of the high Arctic, ranging almost to the northern limits of land around the Northern Hemisphere. Although ptarmigans fly strongly, they remain in the Arctic year-round, undertaking short movements southward in winter or when food is scarce. Unlike the hoofed mammals, they cannot dig through deep snow to find food, so they tend to gather in areas with little snow cover, to*

Rhodostethia rosea (35 cm)

Lagopus mutus (33 cm)

Pagophila eburnea (44 cm)

feed on willow buds, seeds, and berries. Ptarmigans are unusual among grouse in that both parents are involved in the care of the young. While the female incubates the clutch of 8 to 10 eggs, the male stands watch nearby. Later, both parents remain with the brood until the chicks are able to fend for themselves. When a predator is near, their defensive behavior is to remain motionless, flat on the ground, and then spring directly at the head of the intruder. During this moment of confusion, the chicks scatter in all directions and escape.

The gyrfalcon (Falco rusticollis), largest of all falcons, is found throughout the Arctic, but is most common in inland areas. It feeds on large prey—gulls, waterfowl, ground squirrels—but ptarmigans probably make up more than half of its diet. It resides in the Arctic continuously, except when prey populations decrease. At that time, it may undertake short migrations into north temperate regions. Gyrfalcons vary in color from gray-black to almost pure white, the latter form being exceptionally prized by falconers. The smaller peregrine falcon (Falco peregrinus) is also widespread in the north, preferring coastal situations and major rivers, where it feeds mainly on shorebirds and waterfowl. In winter, it leaves the Arctic and migrates south; some birds reach as far as northern South America.

One of the least-known of Arctic birds, Ross' gull (Rhodostethia rosea) is only very rarely seen south of the Arctic Circle. Its main breeding grounds are in the swampy tundra of northeastern Siberia, although it has nested occasionally in Greenland and in the Canadian Arctic. It is the only gull with a wedged-shaped tail, and, during the breeding season, the underparts of the adults are tinged with a delicate pink. After nesting, the birds migrate eastward to northern Alaska, but no one is sure of their whereabouts after October. It is assumed that they spend the winter in the Arctic Ocean, feeding on small fish and crustaceans through openings in the ice.

Summer Birds of the Antarctic

Catharacta maccormicki (52 cm)   **Daption capensis** (41 cm)

Macronectes giganteus (80 cm)   **Oceanites oceanicus** (18 cm)

Most birds of the Antarctic region are seabirds that enter the area in summer to breed and to take advantage of rich feeding opportunities. In the austral autumn they move northward, though remaining in the cooler water zones, for varying distances; most travel toward South America, Africa, and Australia. However, some birds undertake a long and hazardous migration that brings them into the Northern Hemisphere, perhaps as far north as Alaska or Greenland.

Albatrosses are found throughout the southern oceans. Indeed, several species prefer coldwater regions, although no albatross nests as far south as Antarctica. The light-mantled sooty albatross (Phoebetria palpebrata), perhaps the most beautiful of the albatross clan, is the only species that regularly enters the pack ice from its breeding stations on subantarctic islands. Identified by its dark body, pale-gray back, bluish bill, and white eye ring, this albatross can fly hundreds of kilometers from its nesting area in search of food for its chick. It has an exceptionally long wingspread of almost 2 meters, and a long, pointed tail.

With a wingspan well over 2 meters, the southern giant petrel (Macronectes giganteus) is the largest flying seabird of the Antarctic continent. It breeds commonly on the Peninsula and in a few other areas. A more heavy-bodied bird than its close relative, the light-mantled sooty albatross, the color of giant petrels varies from black to gray to almost pure white.

The beautiful Cape pigeon (Daption capensis), is one of the most abundant seabirds in the world. It occupies the pack ice in summer, and in winter wanders widely into warmer seas, occasionally reaching as far north as the Equator.

The Antarctic tern (Sterna vittata) is the only member of its group to breed in the Antarctic, nesting on the Antarctic Peninsula. Not strongly migratory, it spends its entire existence in the vicinity of the pack ice. The very similar Arctic tern (Sterna paradisaea), on the other hand, has the longest migration of any bird. From its Arctic nesting grounds, it migrates across the ocean to the Antarctic, a round-trip of about 30,000 kilometers. These terns winter over the pack ice, most commonly in the Weddell Sea, where they may encounter their southern counterparts. But while

Sterna paradisaea (38 cm)

Chionis alba (41 cm)   *Phoebetria palpebrata* (86 cm)

the Antarctic tern is busily engaged in nesting, the Arctic tern is undergoing an extensive molt that renders it nearly flightless for a brief period. By resting on sea ice and making short flights to feed on the abundant krill, the terns survive quite easily.

With a wingspread of 41 centimeters, and weight of only about 28 grams, Wilson's storm-petrel (Oceanites oceanicus) *is the smallest Antarctic seabird and one of the smallest seabirds in the world. Its migration is no less impressive than that of the Arctic tern. After breeding, these seemingly fragile birds migrate as far as northern Canada, and remain on the high seas all year. Skuas, such as the south polar skua* (Catharacta maccormicki), *are best known as predators on eggs and chicks of penguins. They also prey on petrels and other seabirds, even though they are fully capable of catching fish and scavenging on the open sea. Brown-bodied, with a broad flash of white near the tip of the wing, skuas are known to all who have visited the Antarctic, for they are fierce in defense of their nests and will readily attack and strike humans. In winter, skuas leave the Antarctic and migrate to the North Pacific, apparently over a circular migration route that carries them west to Japan, then to Alaska, and finally, by August or September, south as far as California. During this time, they are found in association with flocks of migrating shearwaters. On the high seas they rarely kill other birds, preferring to harry them until they disgorge their food, which the skua then eats itself.*

The sheathbill (Chionis alba) *is surely the most unusual of Antarctic birds. It resembles a cross between a gull and a pigeon, but has fleshy pinkish skin around the eye and base of the bill. The only bird in the Antarctic region without webbed feet, it is mainly a scavenger, occurring very commonly near seal rookeries and seabird colonies, where it steals eggs and feeds on the leavings of other animals. Sheathbills nest in crevices in the rocks, which they line with feathers. The downy chick's are fed by the adults for a long period before becoming independent. Some sheathbills stay in the Antarctic all year, but most migrate across the Drake Passage to winter on the east coast of South America, as far north as Uruguay.*

Resident Birds of the Antarctic

Pygoscelis antarctica (76 cm)

Aptenodytes forsteri (1.2 m)

Pygoscelis papua (76 cm)

Pygoscelis adeliae (71 cm)

The bird fauna of the Antarctic is neither large nor diverse. Since it consists entirely of species that depend on the sea for survival, most species live and breed only along the coast. The only exceptions are snow petrels and Antarctic petrels, which may fly hundreds of kilometers inland to nest on ice-free cliffs.

More than any other animals, penguins typify the Antarctic region, even though only 4 of the 17 species breed there; the remainder occur in temperate areas of the Southern Hemisphere, and one, the Galápagos penguin (Spheniscus mendiculus), nests as far north as the Equator.

Largest of the living penguins is the emperor (Aptenodytes forsteri), standing over 1 meter high and weighing up to 40 kilograms. It is the only bird that never nests on land, but colonizes on the permanent fast ice that rims the continent.

For the emperor, which breeds in the coldest conditions endured by any bird, the timing of the breeding season is critical. The cycle must begin in the winter, so that the chicks can fledge in the following spring, when conditions for their survival are optimal. Thus, the emperors must remain on the ice in the dark, throughout the entire Antarctic winter. Their adaptations for coping with the environment are still far from understood.

Though the smallest of the true Antarctic penguins, at only 0.7 meters tall, the Adélie penguin (Pygoscelis adeliae) has the widest range, breeding on rocky shores around the continent from the Ross Sea to the tip of the Antarctic Peninsula, and to subantarctic islands as well. It is also by far the most abundant, with many colonies including thousands of pairs.

Summer nesters, Adélies come ashore in October. The first to appear are the males, which return to their nesting sites of the previous year and reassert their claims. Shortly afterward, the females arrive, often returning to their nesting site and mate of past seasons. The brief courtship involves a series of complicated displays, with much wing waving and guttural vocalizations.

Nests are built of small pebbles, which help to keep the eggs above the level of the meltwater. Because pebbles are in short supply, at least one member of the pair remains at the nest at all times to protect the eggs from freezing and pilferage by neighbors. The female lays two

Phalacrocorax atriceps (61 cm) **Thalassoica antarctica** (43 cm)

Pagodroma nivea (34 cm) **Larus dominicanus** (56 cm)

eggs and then, as in other penguins, departs for the sea, leaving the first incubation shift to the male. After about 35 days, the young hatch, and by late January they are ready to go to sea. Some may not return to the land for several years.

Two other species of penguins, more common farther north, reach Antarctica, but nest only on the Antarctic Peninsula and adjacent islands. The chinstrap (Pygoscelis antarctica), known by its distinctive facial markings, is a gregarious bird that often forms huge colonies. The red-billed gentoo (Pygoscelis papua) is a shy creature and often flees at the first sight of humans—unusual behavior for a species that lives in a land free of terrestrial predators. Chinstraps feed mainly on krill, whereas the gentoo has a varied diet consisting mostly of fish and squid.

Except for the penguins, which are flightless, few birds are found in the Antarctic region year-round. The major exceptions, the snow petrel (Pagodroma nivea) and the Antarctic pretrel (Thalassoica antarctica), are seabirds that rarely leave the vicinity of the pack ice.

With its immaculate white plumage and coal black eyes, the snow petrel is among the most striking of all birds. Flying over the pack ice, it appears suddenly against the cobalt blue of the ocean, only to disappear as suddenly among the blue-white of the floes. The brown and white Antarctic petrel occurs in similar situations, but tends to prefer more open areas near the edge of the pack ice. Both species feed mainly on fish or invertebrates, as well as on carrion.

A few other species attempt to overwinter, but even the emperor penguin must move northward to the edge of the ice to find suitable feeding areas. In the milder conditions along the Antarctic Peninsula, a few kelp gulls (Larus dominicanus) or blue-eyed shags (Phalacrocorax atriceps) may persist year-round. The gull is a scavenger, feeding on fish, dead seals, and limpets. The shag is a diving bird that feeds on free-swimming fish.

Seals of the Arctic

Phoca hispida (1.5 m)

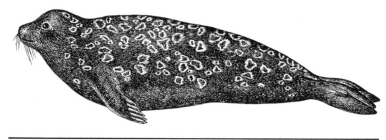

Erignathus barbatus (2.5 m)

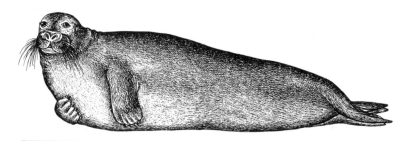

Phoca fasciata (2 m)

The Order Pinnipedia includes three distinct families of marine mammals, each of distinct evolutionary origin. The hair seals (Phocidae) tend to be robust in body form and lack external ears. They are unable to bring their hind flippers forward to aid in terrestrial locomotion, so they are relatively clumsy ashore. They swim by side to side sweeps of the rear flippers and are more aquatic than other pinnipeds; they rarely haul out far from the safety of water. Sea lions and fur seals (Otariidae) are more agile on land because they can bring the rear flippers forward to aid in walking. They swim by flapping the foreflippers in underwater "flight." The remaining family, the Odobenidae, consists of a single species, the walrus—a curious beast that shares some characteristics with each of the other groups.

Most pinnipeds of the Arctic and Antarctic are phocids. This family has representatives in the tropics and in the temperate zones, but its stronghold is in the polar regions.

The ringed seal (Phoca hispida) is named for its coat which has a series of small grayish rings against a darker background. This is the smallest and most widespread of the Arctic seals and a staple food of polar bears and, in some areas, Eskimos. Usually found on shorefast ice, the ring seal population is distributed completely around the Arctic. It maintains breathing holes by using its strong claws to enlarge cracks in the ice. The ringed seal is unique among seals in its use of snow dens among ridges in the ice to shelter and nurse its white-coated pups. A wide variety of fish and invertebrates constitute the ringed seal's diet.

The bearded seal (Erignathus barbatus) generally inhabits pack ice. This largest of Arctic seals (males may weigh as much as 350 kilograms) is a solitary animal. It is found in shallow water over continental shelves, where it feeds on clams, crabs, and other bottom-dwelling invertebrates. Also known as the "square-flipper," the bearded seal can be recognized by its coat, relatively small head, and the abundant whiskers which give it a "bearded" look. In spring, males are very vocal, "singing" underwater in territorial display. Eskimos use its thick hide for boot soles, sledge traces, and rope.

The ribbon seal (Phoca fasciata) and the harp seal (Phoca groenlandica) are the most pelagic of Arctic seals. Both are boldly

Phoca groenlandica (2 m)

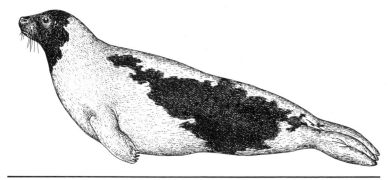

Cystophora cristata (2.5 m)

Odobenus rosmarus (4 m)

patterned, occur mainly in loose pack ice, and eat mostly fish and squid. The ribbon seal is restricted to the Bering and Okhotsk seas. The pups, which are white at birth, require 3 years to attain adult coloration. The harp seal, like the ribbon seal, breeds on the open sea ice, congregating in specific areas, a habit that facilitates commercial hunting; the quarry is the newborn pup, whose brilliant white fur is highly prized. Although this seal is extremely vocal underwater, its name is not derived from its singing ability but from the dark, V-shaped marking on the back. It is restricted to the Atlantic portion of the Arctic region—from Newfoundland to western Russia. After the breeding season, the seals move northward with the retreating ice.

Also restricted to the Atlantic area is the hooded seal, or bladdernose (Cystophora cristata). It is highly pelagic and breeds on floes near the edge of the pack. This large seal has a spotted coat and remarkable nose that is probably used in courtship or threat displays. Adult males can inflate the entire nose or just the septum (which divides the nostrils) into a large, red "balloon." Males weigh about as much as bearded seals; females are much smaller.

The walrus (Odobenus rosmarus) is unique. Like the hair seals, it is earless, but like the sea lions it is able to bring its hind flippers under its body to aid in walking on land. Its immense size (males weigh as much as 1,700 kilograms), relatively small head, long tusks, and whiskered muzzle give it an appearance totally unlike that of any other animal. These are social animals, usually occurring in large herds. They breed on the ice in winter. In summer, many of the males separate from the rest of the herd and haul out on land. Although found in both Atlantic and Pacific sectors of the Arctic, walruses are far commoner in the latter; they winter in the Bering Sea and migrate north to summer in the Chukchi Sea. They are bottom feeders, and are thus restricted to continental shelf waters, where they consume clams and other invertebrates.

Seals of the Antarctic

Arctocephalus gazella (2.5 m)

Mirounga leonina (6 m)

Leptonychotoes weddelli (3 m)

There are no terrestrial mammals in the Antarctic, but marine mammals are extremely abundant. Of the six species of seals that range south of the Antarctic convergence, two, the Kerguelen fur seal (Arctocephalus gazella) and the southern elephant seal (Mirounga leonina) live mainly on subantarctic or Antarctic islands, such as South Georgia and the South Shetlands. Each of the four species of true Antarctic seals, called lobodontines, is highly distinctive in body form, color, and habits, and each tends to occupy a different type of ice habitat, although there is much overlap. The Weddell seal (Leptonychtoes weddelli) has the southernmost breeding area of any mammal in the world. It lives almost exclusively in the fast ice zone and breeds as far south as 78° south latitude. A large, spotted seal, it feeds mainly on bottom-dwelling fish and invertebrates. Highly vocal, this seal has many distinctive calls. During the Antarctic spring, large groups of Weddell seals appear in areas where tidal cracks form in the ice. These are their pupping areas. The seals are generally docile and very easily approached, and marking and tagging have revealed that the same animals may return year after year to the same place. During the winter, Weddell seals apparently spend most of their time in the water. They breathe through cracks in the ice or make breathing holes by sawing away at the ice with their forward-pointing upper incisors and canines. Tooth wear and dental complication from such activities may be an occasional cause of death.

Smallest of the Antarctic seals, the Ross seal (Ommatophoca rossi) generally lives in heavy pack ice, where there is little open water; in only one area, near the eastern Weddell Sea, are they found in open pack ice. Because of its inaccessible habitat, it has remained the least studied of the Antarctic seals. It was long considered a very rare species, but, as modern icebreakers have been able to survey this habitat on a regular basis, we have learned that it is probably no less common than the ubiquitous leopard seal. Named for James Ross, commander of a 3-year British expedition to the Antarctic from 1839 to 1841, this seal is usually seen resting alone, or occasionally in small groups on the ice pack. Apparently it feeds mainly on squid or other cephalopods. Its short face, tiny

Ommatophoca rossi (2 m)

Lobodon carcinophagus (1.8 m)

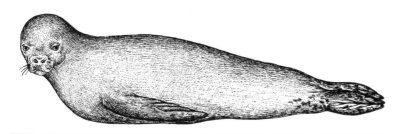

Hydrurga leptonyx (3.5 m)

teeth, and unusual posture when disturbed—upright with head thrown back—make it easily recognizable. It is also known for its distinctive warbling or chugging vocalizations, which may be used in underwater communication.

By far the most numerous seal in the Antarctic waters and, indeed, the most abundant seal in the world, is the crabeater (Lobodon carcinophagus). *Its total population has been estimated at 15 to 30 million; such estimates are open to question however, since crabeaters are not uniformly distributed around the continent. In any event, they are extremely common, comprising perhaps 95 percent of the Antarctic seal population. They live in the open pack ice, where the ice cover varies from 30 to 70 percent. Typically they are seen loafing, singly or in groups of 3 to 4, on small floes. Almost their entire diet consists of krill, which, it is thought, they obtain by straining water through their lobed teeth; however this feeding behavior remains questionable. With long muzzles and a silvery-tan coat with few spots, crabeaters have a doglike visage. They are preyed on by leopard seals and killer whales and many bear scars from their encounters with these predators.*

A powerful predator, with a weight exceeding 450 kilograms, the leopard seal (Hydrurga leptonyx) *is the longest of the true Antarctic seals. It is also the most widely distributed and may occur anywhere from the edge of the continent to the edge of the pack ice, though it prefers open pack ice. In winter, some leopard seals stray as far north as New Zealand and Australia; these are usually young animals. Leopard seals eat a wide variety of animals. Although they frequently feed on other seals and penguins, which they will pursue through ice floes as well as open water, perhaps one-third of their diet consists of fish and krill. A solitary animal, it is commonly seen resting on floes in the open pack, not far from crabeaters and penguin colonies. With its spotted coat, slender build, and reptilian head and neck, it is unmistakable.*

Whales in Arctic Waters

Delphinapterus leucas (5 m)

Balaena mysticetus (18 m)

Hyperoodon ampullatus (12 m)

Most widespread of the northern toothed whales is the belukha, or white whale (Delphinapterus leucas). *Young belukhas are dark grayish, and several years pass before they attain adult coloration. Highly social, the belukha often congregates in herds of several hundred to several thousand individuals. Unlike most other whales, they tolerate fresh water and often enter rivers to feed. They consume a wide variety of fish and invertebrates. Migratory belukhas remain in high Arctic waters until early fall, then gradually move southward away from the heavy ice to loose ice. Some distinct, small populations probably never leave southern Alaska, the Baltic sea, and the Gulf of St. Lawrence.*

Only one species of baleen whale, the bowhead (Balaena mysticetus), *inhabits polar regions year-round. In summer, bowheads feed mainly near the ice front or inshore, ranging eastward to the Canadian Beaufort Sea and westward to Siberia. In fall they move south, often very close to shore, into the Bering Sea. On returning northward in spring, most follow a large opening in the ice near shore called the* flaw zone. *The presence of long stretches of open water is not essential to bowheads, however, as these massive beasts can push their heads or bodies through half a meter or more of solid ice to gain breathing space.*

Known by its pointed snout and high, dome-shaped forehead, the little-studied bottlenose whale (Hyperoodon ampullatus) *was formerly a fairly common species. More abundant in the Atlantic than in the Pacific, the species occurs widely in Arctic waters as well as in the cold North Atlantic. In the bottlenose, as in many other toothed whales, males are larger than females.*

The narwhal (Monodon monoceros) *is appropriately named;* Monodon *means "one tooth." Present in males, and growing continuously for the whale's entire life, the tooth is probably used in setting up dominance hierarchies among males. But this, like most of what is believed of the narwhal, is only speculative. Like most other toothed whales, narwhals are social animals, usually occurring in groups of from 3 to 12 individuals. They may dive over 300 meters in pursuit of their prey, which consists mostly of squid. This is the most northerly*

Monodon monoceros (5 m)

Eschrictius robustus (15 m)

Balaenoptera physalus (21 m)

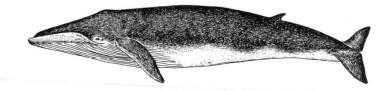

of toothed whales, year-round; it is almost always found in the immediate vicinity of ice. Even in winter it rarely moves far from the ice, and then only far enough to ensure open water for breathing.

The gray whale (Eschrictius robustus) is the sole representative of a rather primitive group of whales. It lacks the extensive series of throat grooves and the dorsal fin of the rorquals and the massive head of the right whales. Instead, it is short-faced, with only two to three short throat grooves and has a series of bumps, or "knuckles" on its back. It undertakes the most extensive annual migration of any mammal. It enters Arctic waters in May, ranging north into the Chukchi Sea, where it remains until late fall. During its stay, it feeds almost constantly. Its short, thick baleen is adapted for filtering crustaceans, mostly amphipods, that it takes from the bottom. The muddy trails of the whales in shallow water are obvious indicators of their feeding activity. In October, they head south to the shallow lagoons of Baja California, where they court and calve. Along for the ride are two "hitchhikers," whale barnacles and whale lice, which congregate on the head near the blowholes.

They swim continuously, day and night, at 6 to 8 kilometers per hour, until they reach the breeding grounds, where the 4.3-meter calves are born. By late March, they begin the return trip of a migration that will take them a total of 16,000 kilometers. Whales on the northward journey weigh about 30 percent less than those going south and probably do not feed to any great extent in the 6 months they spend away from Arctic seas.

Almost any of the other baleen whales may occasionally enter the Arctic. Perhaps the most regular summer visitor is the giant fin whale, or finback (Balaenoptera physalus), which attains a length of 25 meters. It is a fairly common species in the North Atlantic, off eastern Canada and near Greenland and Iceland. It also enters the Bering Sea, but rarely when sea ice is present.

Eubalaena glacialis (12–15 m)

Megaptera novaeangliae (13–15 m)

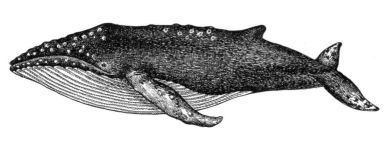

Balaenoptera musculus (29 m)

The southern right whales (Eubalaena glacialis) *have massive heads that make up more than one-fourth of their total length. They are broad-backed, lack dorsal fins, and have very long, slender baleen plates. They can also be recognized by the low, broad, V-shaped spout. During courtship, they leap clear of the water repeatedly, or perform head-stands with their flukes waving back and forth in the air. Breeding occurs in shallow coastal bays in June or July, and by late September the southern right whales are on their way to the austral feeding grounds.*

The humpbacked whale (Megaptera novaeangliae) *is easily identified by its highly elongated flippers that exceed one-quarter the length of its body, and by its oddly shaped, broad-based dorsal fin. Its name derives from its habit of arching its back sharply prior to a deep dive, after which it tosses its flukes high into the air. It ranges worldwide, breeds in coastal waters, and often summers in the vicinity of oceanic islands, such as Bermuda or Hawaii. Southern Hemisphere populations undergo regular annual migrations from South America, New Zealand, and Australia into Antarctic waters each spring.*

The blue whale (Balaeoptera musculus) *can be recognized by its size—it is the largest of all creatures that have ever lived—and by its spotted blue-gray coloration, tiny dorsal fin placed far to the rear, and very high, single spout. It is generally solitary, or occurs in small groups. Although blue whales are highly migratory, their breeding grounds are not known. Presumably they breed in mid-ocean in temperate seas. The calves are 7 to 8 meters long at birth and grow rapidly because of the high fat content of the mother's milk. Breeding begins from age 10 to 20, and some individuals live as long as 90 years.*

The sei (Balaenoptera borealis) *is most abundant in subantarctic waters and rarely enters the pack ice. It feeds mainly on fast-swimming prey, particularly herring-like fishes and other small schooling species.*

The minke whale (Balaenoptera acutorostrata) *is the smallest of the baleen whales in the Antarctic but by far the most common. A fast-swimming whale, it can be recognized by its pointed dorsal fin, blackish coloration, and the white bands across its flippers. It is most commonly found well*

Balaenoptera borealis (15–18 m)

within the pack-ice zone, often many miles from any extensive stretch of open water. The minke is very inquisitive, well known for its habit of approaching boats. Despite its abundance, the minke's annual movements are still largely a mystery.

The strikingly marked killer whale (Orcinus orca) is found in all oceans, but is most common in cool or cold waters. A social animal, it moves about in small family groups of 1 or 2 males and several females and calves. Herds as large as several hundred have been reported, but such groupings are rare. Males are much larger than females and are easily recognized by the height of their huge dorsal fin, which may extend 1.8 meters above the back. This is the largest of all carnivores. An opportunistic feeder, it preys mainly on fish and seals; but, as its name implies, it will attack even the largest whales. In the Antarctic, killer whales follow leads through the ice to the very edge of the continent; penguins, crabeater seals, and minke whales, as well as fish, are important components of its diet.

Balaenoptera acutorostrata (10 m)

Orcinus orca (8 m)

Fishes of the Arctic

Somniosus microcephalus (6.5 m)

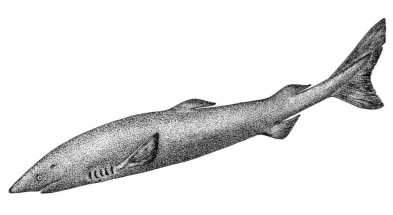

Cottunculus microps (30 cm)

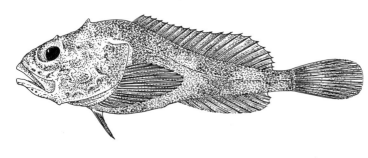

Stenodus leucichthys (150 cm)

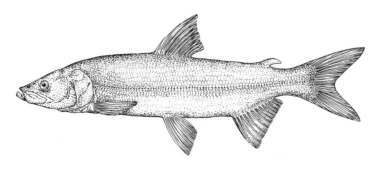

Sharks are members of a group of fishes called the Chondrichthyes, meaning "cartilagenous fish"; they have no bones in their skeletons and are more primitive than the teleosts, or bony fishes. The Greenland shark (Somniosus microcephalus) is the largest species of dogfish shark (Squalidae), reaching a length of over 6½ meters. It is the most northerly member of its family, which though nearly worldwide in distribution, is not found in the Antarctic. The Greenland shark is almost entirely an Arctic species, only rarely straying into more temperate waters, and then it occurs only in very deep, cold waters at depths of 600 meters. In the Arctic it is often seen at the surface. The Greenland shark feeds on seals, seabirds, squids, porpoises, and whales. At one time, it was taken commercially off the northern coast of Greenland. Its liver oil was used for fuel, and its dried flesh for dog food—when not dried, its flesh is supposedly poisonous to dogs and humans.

The sculpins (Cottidae) constitute a large family of fishes that are found only in the Northern Hemisphere. There are both freshwater and marine representatives. Sculpins are small- to medium-sized fishes, reaching over 30 centimeters in length. Most species inhabit shallow water, and all live and feed on the bottom. The Arctic sculpin (Cottunculus microps) is the most northerly species, occurring chiefly in Arctic waters, but occasionally straying farther south into temperate waters. The Arctic sculpin lives in deeper water than do most other members of its family; it has been caught at depths of 800 meters.

The whitefishes (Coregonidae) are a widely distributed group of fishes and are restricted to the Northern Hemisphere. They are closely related to the Salmonidae —trouts, salmons, and chars. (In fact, whitefishes are sometimes considered members of the Salmonidae.) The inconnu (Stenodus leucichthys) is the most northern, and probably the largest species of whitefish, reaching a length of over 150 centimeters and a weight of over 40 kilograms. Inconnu, like all other whitefish, are edible, and are fished wherever they occur. The inconnu lives mainly in deep, murky rivers and lakes, but many populations are migratory and spend part of their lifetime in the Arctic Ocean. They spawn in the autumn far upstream in clear, shallow water. Adult

Salvelinus alpinus (96 cm)

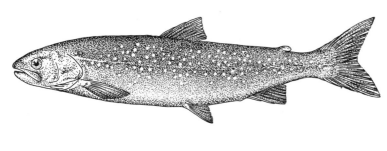

Boreogadus saida (46 cm)

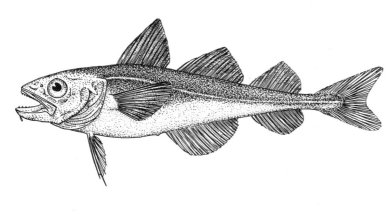

Dallia pectoralis (20 cm)

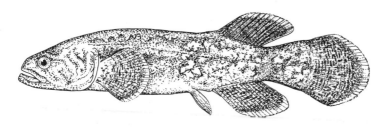

inconnu are highly predatory, feeding almost exclusively on other fish. This species was named by early French explorers in the far northern areas. In French, inconnu means "unknown": the species was literally unknown farther south. The Arctic char (Salvelinus alpinus), like its relatives the trouts and salmons, spawns in shallow, clear, cold streams and migrates downstream to the open sea—in this case to the Arctic Ocean. However, in some places the Arctic char spends its entire lifetime in cool, deep lakes where it has lived isolated since the retreat of the glaciers after the last Ice Age. It grows to a length of over 96 centimeters and a weight of over 12 kilograms. As an adult, the Arctic char is highly predaceous, feeding principally on other fishes. The young fish feed mainly on insects and small crustaceans. Codfishes (Gadidae) are a large marine group found mainly in the Northern Hemisphere, although a few species range south of the Equator, and one species is found in fresh water.

Codfishes are one of the most commercially important groups of fishes, although the Arctic cod (Boreogadus saida) is not fished commercially. This is due both to its extreme northern range and to its small size—less than 46 centimeters. The Arctic cod is found almost exclusively in the Arctic Ocean and is often seen schooling at the surface around ice floes. It is very common and is a principal food of seals, polar bears, birds, and some whales. The Arctic cod feeds mainly on invertebrates.

The blackfish (Dallia pectoralis) is the largest and northernmost member of its family (Umbridae), and reaches a length of 20 centimeters. The Umbridae is a strictly Northern Hemisphere family, with species found in both North America and Eurasia. The blackfish is fairly common in the streams, marshes, and lakes of the tundra. It is well-adapted to this environment, being able to live for long periods of time under the ice, where there is almost no oxygen. At one time, blackfish were exploited for use as dog food. They breed in July, during the Arctic summer, and feed mainly on insects, small crustaceans, and snails. Members of the Umbridae family are closely related to pikes and pickerels (Esocidae), another Northern Hemisphere group.

Fishes of the Antarctic

Channichthys rhinoceratus (60 cm)

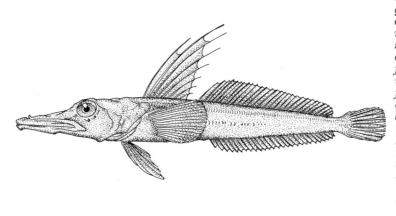

Trematomus bernacchii (35 cm)

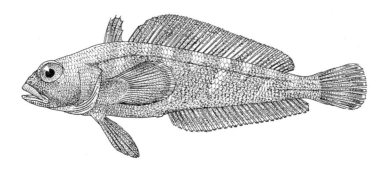

Pleuragramma antarcticum (20 cm)

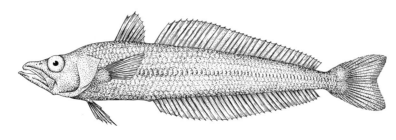

The white-blooded fishes (*Channichthyidae*) constitute a group of 13 species of relatively common fishes. They are restricted to the Antarctic and subantarctic region, living at depths of 5 to 340 meters. They feed off the bottom on small invertebrates. Most white-blooded fishes are medium-sized, reaching a length of 60 centimeters. Some, like the icefish (Channichthys rhinoceratus), are quite beautiful, having an iridescent purple color. The most interesting feature of the white-blooded fishes is the characteristic for which they are named—the lack of red blood cells which contain the red, oxygen-carrying hemoglobin; their blood is clear or whitish. Oxygen is carried in the blood plasma rather than the hemoglobin. Because this is not an energy-efficient way of transporting oxygen through their bodies, it is easy to understand why white-blooded fishes are sedentary. This lack of red blood was first observed by whalers, but scientists remained skeptical for a long time. White-blooded fishes are believed to be close relatives of the Antarctic "cods."

Antarctic cods (*Nototheniidae*) are also confined to the Antarctic and subantarctic regions. There are approximately 32 species of Antarctic cods; they are the most abundant group of fishes in the region. These fishes are an important link in the Antarctic food chain; they are the main source of food for several species of penguins and seals. They are most closely related to the weever fishes (Suborder Trachinoidea) both groups being subgroups of the perchlike fishes (Order Percomorpha). The Antarctic cods are not related to the true cods (Gadidae) of the Northern Hemisphere. Trematomus bernacchi is an Antarctic cod found all around the Antarctic continental shelf at depths of 700 meters. It lives on the bottom and feeds mainly on invertebrates such as worms, mollusks, and crustaceans. It is reddish-brown in color, and reaches a length of 35 centimeters.

The Antarctic herring (Pleuragramma antarcticum) is a small fish, reaching only 20 centimeters in length. Records from the Ross Sea indicate that it is probably the most common species of fish in the Antarctic. This is the only nototheniid that is wholly pelagic; it lives in midwater at depths of 150 to 500 meters. The young, however, usually live closer to the surface

Dissostichus mawoni (1.5 m)

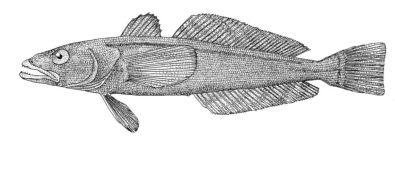

Pogonophryne marmoratus (20 cm)

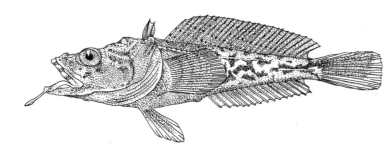

Bathydraco marri (40 cm)

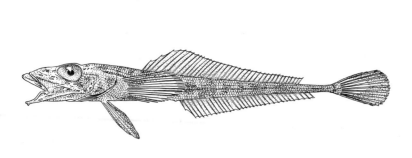

and have been caught at depths of 80 meters.

The giant Antarctic cod (Dissostichus mawsoni) *is the largest of the Antarctic cods, reaching a length of over 1.5 meters. Quite common and widely distributed over the Antarctic region, this fish normally lives in depths of 20 to 200 meters, where it lives close to, and feeds off, the ocean bottom. The Antarctic sculpins (Harpagiferidae) are a family of fishes closely related to the Antarctic cods, and are found only in the Antarctic and subantarctic region. The marble plunder fish (Pogonophryne marmoratus) is one of 10 species of Antarctic sculpins. These fish reach lengths of up to 20 centimeters. Antarctic "sculpins" are found in very shallow water, under or around rocks or clumps of algae on the bottom. Most species have a barbel under the chin, which scientists believe is used as a lure to prey. In overall appearance, as well as behavior, the Antarctic sculpins resemble true sculpins (Cottidae) of the Northern Hemisphere, but the two families are unrelated. Dragonfishes (Bathydraconidae) are a relatively rare group of fishes that are restricted to the Antarctic. They live in relatively deep water. Some, like the deepwater dragonfish (Bathydraco marri), have been caught at depths of 2,650 meters. Dragonfishes are closely related to Antarctic cods and sculpins. They reach a length of approximately 40 centimeters. Dragonfishes are known to be bottom-dwellers, but little else is known of their life history or habits.*

Glossary

Adaptive strategy. The means by which a species adjusts, or adapts, to its environment.

Anchor ice. Ice that forms on the seafloor. Anchor ice may form around organisms and then float to the surface, raising the organisms from the bottom, a process called *anchor stripping.*

Antarctic Circle. A parallel of latitude that is approximately 66 degrees, 33 minutes south of the Equator, and which defines the northern limit of the Antarctic zone (astronomically, not biologically.)

Antarctic convergence. A circumpolar region where surface waters, moving in a southerly direction, meet Antarctic surface waters moving north. These water masses converge and sink at the Antarctic convergence. The Antarctic convergence is an important biogeographic feature of the Southern Hemisphere, occurring in or near 50 to 60 degrees south latitude. It can be traced around the world in open water between Antarctica and Africa, Australia, and South America.

Antarctic region. The area of the Earth south of the Antarctic convergence.

Antifreeze. A substance that prevents liquid from freezing at low temperatures. Certain Antarctic fishes have such sugar-protein substances in their blood.

Arctic Basin. That part of the deep world ocean that occurs within the Arctic region.

Arctic Circle. A parallel of latitude that is approximately 66 degrees, 33 minutes north of the Equator, and that defines the southern limit of the Arctic zone.

Arctic region. The area of the Northern Hemisphere in which the mean temperature during the warmest month of the year is 10°C or lower.

Aurora. A luminous atmospheric phenomenon called the northern (aurora borealis) or southern lights (aurora australis), attributed to electrical phenomena that charge particles in the upper atmosphere, radiating from the northern or southern magnetic pole.

Axial poles. The poles of the true axis of the Earth, as opposed to the magnetic poles. The north and south poles are the axial poles of the Earth.

Benthos. The floor of a sea or ocean.

Beringia. The Bering-Chukchi Sea continental shelf, formerly the land bridge between Asia and the Americas.

Bering Sea. A body of water bounded by Siberia, Alaska, the Aleutian Islands, and the Bering Strait.

Biomass. The amount of living material in a given area expressed as weight or volume.

Biome. The largest of all ecological units, made up of the plants and animals in a broad region of the Earth. Each biome is kept distinct from the others by physical factors such as temperature, rainfall, salinity, light intensity, and the availability of nutrients.

Chukchi Sea. An Arctic sea between the coast of Siberia and the Arctic rim of North America, the northern boundary being the edge of the continental shelf running from Point Barrow to 75 degrees north, the latitude of Wrangel Island. The western boundary is at about Wrangel Island to Cape Yakan on the Russian mainland.

Continental shelf. Land that extends from a continent beneath the sea surface in relatively shallow water. Beyond the shelf is a continental slope, where the seafloor descends to the ocean's depths.

Convergent evolution. The evolution of similar anatomical or physiological traits in widely different and otherwise unrelated organisms.

Copepod. A crustacean having four or five pairs of oar-like legs. It is common among the zooplankton and usually feeds on phytoplankton.

Detritus. Finely divided, finely particulate organic matter.

Diatom. A microscopic, planktonic, unicellular alga with mineralized cell walls containing silicon. Deposits of the silicious walls of diatoms form large deposits of diatomaceous earth. Diatoms are primary producers in marine waters and also occur in benthic habitats in shallow water.

Echolocation. A means by which distances are judged by the time between sound emission and the sensing of an echo. Large marine mammals produce underwater sounds, often high in pitch, that bounce back from surfaces around them. They use echolocation when pursuing prey and as a means of avoiding obstacles.

Ecotone. A boundary or zone of intergradation between two ecosystems.

Enzymes. Substances in living organisms that determine biochemical reactions and thus control the dynamic events of the life process. Enzymes are responsible for the digestion of food, the contraction of muscles, the clotting of blood, and countless other processes.

Felsenmeer. A German term that refers to *talus*, or coarse and angular rock rubble, most often derived from and accumulated at the base of a cliff or slope.

Firn. Thawed and refrozen consolidated snow that is less white and more dense than normal snow. Firn is snow that is becoming nonpermeable and that is on the way to becoming solid glacial ice.

Fjord. A narrow coastal valley flooded by the sea. Fjords are commonly formed by glaciers and may be over 1,000 meters deep.

Floe. A mass of floating pack ice usually more than 10 meters across.

Glacier. A large mass of ice formed by the compaction of snow whose weight can force it to move. Approximately 10 percent of the Earth's surface is covered by glaciers, which are found on all continents except Australia.

Gondwanaland. A very large landmass that formerly existed in the Southern Hemisphere, which, according to modern concepts of continental drift, began to break up about 130 million years ago and whose fragments form the present-day continents of South America, Africa, Australia, Antarctica, and the subcontinent of India.

Grease ice. Ice formed at the sea surface, producing a slush with a slightly oily appearance.

Gray ice. Recently formed ice, 10 to 15 centimeters thick.

Ice Age. A period dominated by the accumulation of large terrestrial ice masses. An ice age occurred during the Permian period (300 to 250 million years ago), and another is taking place now.

Iceberg. A large, floating mass of ice, often rising to a great height above the water, commonly derived from a glacier or an ice shelf.

Krill. A crustacean commonly found in great abundance in Antarctic waters. Krill (*Euphausia superba*), feed on phytoplankton and form the principal food of baleen whales.

Laurentide Ice Sheet. A major ice mass that once covered North America east of the Rockies from the Arctic Ocean to a line extending from New York to Columbus, Ohio, and the Dakotas.

Lead. A channel of open water that results when sea ice parts.

Lichen. A composite plant consisting of a fungus and one or more kinds of algae, living together and having a characteristic macroscopic form. Lichens can live under extremely severe conditions and are a major component of Arctic and Antarctic land vegetation.

Magnetic pole. One of two points near opposite ends of a magnet where the magnetic intensity is the greatest. Magnetic lines of force leave the magnet at the positive, or north-seeking, pole and enter at the negative, or south-seeking, pole.

Malthusian. Pertaining to the mathematical theory of Thomas P. Malthus that a population of animals tends to increase faster than its food supply, unless that population is checked by famine, disease, or natural predators.

McMurdo Sound. A region in the western Ross Sea that is usually free of pack ice in late summer and that has served as a staging point for the establishment of a major United States scientific station, and from which inland expeditions are launched.

Niche. The way of life of a species, in terms of where it lives, when it is active, and what it contributes as either a primary producer or a consumer in the food web.

Nunatak. An island of ice-free rock or land projecting out through an ice mass.

Orthogenic soil. Soil that is derived from bird droppings. Orthogenic soil is usually coarse and dark.

Pack ice. A large accumulation of densely packed ice floes pushed together by wind or currents.

Pancake ice. Small pieces of ice with raised edges that look like lily pads, formed when pieces of frozen ice collide as the result of water movement. These pieces are usually less than 10 meters in diameter.

Pangaea. A hypothetical continent proposed by the German meteorologist Alfred Wegener. Wegener suggested that all of the Earth's present continents were once part of a single, giant continental land mass that he called *Pangaea*. The remainder of the globe was covered by a single sea called *Panthalassa*. According to Wegener's continental-drift hypothesis, Pangaea cracked apart and, via continental drift, became the continents that we know today.

Parasitism. An association between two different species in which one, the parasite, benefits at the expense of the host.

Pelagic. Occupying the open sea, far from shore. Pelagic animals depend on the photosynthetic production of phytoplankton for their food.

Permafrost. Permanently frozen layer of earth that may or may not contain ice.

Photosynthesis. The process by which the energy of sunlight is used by green plants to produce sugars and starches from carbon dioxide and water.

Phytoplankton. Floating, usually microscopic plant life that occurs in fresh and marine waters. Phytoplankton form the basis for all marine food webs; they are the primary producers of organic material.

Pingo. A large frost mound that is often conical and covered with soil. It is raised, in part, by the pressure of ice freezing within or below the permafrost in Arctic regions. The crest of a pingo sometimes ruptures or collapses when the ice melts and forms a star-shaped crater. A pingo can resemble a small volcano; some can be 30 to 50 meters high and up to 400 meters in diameter.

Pinnipeds. Marine mammals such as seals, sea lions, and walruses. These animals have flipper–like feet and are often abundant in polar regions.

Plate tectonics. The movement of the crustal plates of the Earth, that bear the continents. As the crustal plates move, the continents drift apart; continental drift is thus a result of the movement of the Earth's crust.

Polynya. A Russian term that refers to a region of open water surrounded by sea ice. One side of a polynya may be the coast. Polynyas also occur in pack ice.

Procaryote. An organism lacking a membrane-bound nucleus within its cell. Examples are the bacteria and the blue-green algae. Procaryotes are thought to be the oldest form of life still extant.

Pyramid. A graphic representation of the biomass or numerical relationships among organisms in an ecosystem, in which the primary producers have the largest population and are considered the base of the pyramid, and in which the population decreases with each level of consumers until one reaches the highest level, which has the smallest population and is considered the apex of the pyramid.

Refugium. An isolated area that has undergone little environmental change over a long period of time, thereby allowing a fauna and flora to persist long after similar habitats have been eliminated in the surrounding areas. A refugium might be an ice-free area where plants and animals persisted during a glacial time and which later served as a center of distribution for the repopulation of the area when conditions improved.

Ross Sea. A region of the Pacific Ocean discovered in 1841 by Sir James Clark Ross, a British explorer. The Ross Sea lies between Victoria Land and Marie Byrd Land off the coast of Antarctica.

Sea ice. Ice that forms when sea water freezes, as distinguished from glacier ice or icebergs, which are frozen fresh water.

Shorefast ice. Sea ice that is attached to the shore, also called fast ice.

Southern Ocean. That region of the world ocean where the Atlantic, Indian, and Pacific oceans are contiguous. The Southern Ocean surrounds Antarctica.

Subantarctic. Adjacent to the Antarctic; that region north of the Antarctic convergence and south of the subtropical convergence.

Subarctic. Adjacent to the Arctic region. The subarctic includes the north Pacific in the Bering Sea and the North Atlantic north of Labrador, Iceland, and Norway.

Symbiotic species. Two species living together in an association in which both benefit, or in which one of the pair may be harmed.

Treeline. The level on a mountain, or latitude on a continent, above which no trees grow. In the Arctic there is a treeline north of which trees do not occur, but where tundra vegetation does exist.

Trophic level. A component of an ecological community defined by the means in which organisms in it obtain energy. The primary trophic level is occupied by plants that manufacture their own food, while herbivores occupy a secondary trophic level. Carnivores occupy the highest trophic level, feeding on the herbivores.

Tundra. Treeless land beyond the northernmost limits of the forests, or above the treeline. Tundra is well-developed in North America and Eurasia, where a great deal of subpolar land mass exists.

Zooplankton. Minute animals that are free-swimming or free-floating in an aquatic habitat, such as an ocean or a lake.

Index

Page numbers in boldface type indicate illustrations

229